Help!

The Quick Guide to First Aid for Your Cat

Michelle Bamberger, DVM

HOWELL
BOOK
HOUSE

New York

Howell Book House
A Simon & Schuster Macmillan Company
1633 Broadway
New York, NY 10019

Library of Congress Cataloging-in-Publication Data
Bamberger, Michelle.
    Help! : the quick guide to first aid for your cat / by Michelle Bamberger
    p. cm.
Includes bibliographical references and index.
ISBN 0-87605-794-6
    1. Cats—Wounds and injuries—Treatment—Handbooks, manuals, etc.   2. Cats—
Diseases—Treatment—Handbooks, manuals, etc.   3. Veterinary emergencies—Hand-
books, manuals, etc.   4. First aid for animals—Handbooks, manuals, etc.   I. Title.
SF985.B36   1995
636.8'08960252—dc20   94-37313
    CIP

Manufactured in the United States of America
10 9 8 7 6 5 4 3

Book design by Kris Tobiassen

For Jean Evans and her cats

Contents

Acknowledgments

C ats can be our best friends, but are not often known to be helpful. With a little encouragement, my cat Apricot tolerated a two-hour photo session, being held, posed, wrapped with bandages and playing dead. Besides Apricot, the illustrations would not have been possible without the assistance of Dr. Nena Winand, who not only posed for some pictures with her own cat, Tai Tai, but also managed to convince Apricot to remain calm during the entire session. Marcy Zingler, my editor at Howell, has shown continued interest in and enthusiasm for this book. Dr. James Richards, extension veterinarian for the Cornell Feline Health Center, and Dr. Susan Begg, small animal practitioner and firefighter, took time away from their own busy schedules to read through an initial draft and make helpful comments and suggestions. Finally, I am indebted to Professor Robert Oswald for reading through an initial draft, but most of all, for tending our two sons, Benjamin and Aaron, for extended periods of time so that I could write this book.

Michelle Bamberger, DVM
Ithaca, New York

Introduction

This book is written for cat owners who want to know how to act responsibly in an emergency. It is not meant to replace veterinarians; rather, it attempts to make cat owners more aware of how to approach emergencies and how to handle them effectively until a veterinarian can be reached.

I have taught first aid to pet owners, SPCA personnel and animal health technicians. Since I was unable to recommend a book that specifically covers emergency care in an easy-to-understand, thorough, and illustrated manner, I decided to write one. This book is an outgrowth of that course and contains many of the illustrations I used to describe first aid techniques to my students.

I recommend that you begin by reading the first two chapters. Together, these chapters describe a general approach that can be used in all emergencies. In addition, Chapter 1 describes basic life-saving techniques, while Chapter 2 lists first aid for specific conditions you might find while examining your cat. Typical emergencies are discussed in Chapter 3. *Don't wait until the emergency occurs to read this chapter.* Acquaint yourself with the signs and first aid for each emergency so that if one does occur, you will be able to recognize it and will have an idea of what steps to take. Wound and fracture care are described in Chapter 4. In this chapter, bandages for different parts of the body are illustrated step by step. Finally, Chapter 5 gives you a chance to encounter some real-life emergencies and decide what to do (the answers are in Appendix 3).

First Aid Supplies

The following is a list of first aid supplies that you should have available in your home:

Adhesive tape
Blankets
Board or window screen
Bucket
Cardboard boxes (heavy and
    light)
Cotton balls
Cotton roll
Cotton swabs
Cup
Gauze roll
Masking tape
Medications (see Appendix 2
    for use and dosages)

- Activated charcoal
- Antibiotic ointment
    (Neosporin® or
    Bacitracin)

- Hydrogen peroxide
    (3 percent)
- Syrup of ipecac
- Vegetable or mineral oil

Medicine dropper
Pads (preferably nonstick)
Pencil
Scissors
Sheets (bed)
Soap
Thermometer (preferably
digital)
Tongue depressors
Towels
Tweezers
Washcloth

What to Do First:
Basic Life-Saving Techniques

I f you found your cat injured and unable to move, would you know what to do first? In an emergency such as this, your cat may be suffering from more than one type of injury.

If the cat were hit by a car, you might notice a few problems right away: a large bleeding wound on the back and a fractured hind leg. On further examination, you discover your cat is in shock and probably has internal injuries. Your knowledge of what to do first and use of standard first-aid techniques will dramatically affect your cat's recovery.

In this chapter, you will learn the basic steps used to approach all emergencies and the first-aid methods for the most life-threatening situations. Section 1 will cover triage, which is the art of determining the problems and then sorting them according to severity. Section 2 will discuss restraint and transport; these techniques are often necessary before any first aid can be given. In Sections 3 through 6, I will explain and illustrate first-aid methods used to treat extreme emergency conditions: cardiopulmonary failure, drowning, choking, shock, and severe bleeding.

Whatever the emergency, having your cat evaluated by your veterinarian is critical. You may administer first aid on the way to see the veterinarian. Alternatively, you may bring your cat in for a checkup after the animal's condition is stabilized. Even if you feel your cat has completely recovered, you should call a veterinarian and describe the emergency. Your veterinarian may be able to give you advice and suggestions to help your cat make an even quicker recovery. Remember that, whenever possible, you should call ahead before bringing your cat to an emergency clinic or veterinary hospital. Doing this will allow the staff time to prepare for your cat's arrival.

SECTION 1: TRIAGE

Assessing Your Cat

Before taking any action in an emergency, make sure the environment is safe. For example, if the emergency takes place on a busy road, in a burning building, or near electrical hazards, you will have to move your cat to a safer location before doing anything else. And if your cat is uncooperative, you will have to provide some form of restraint before you can start first aid (see Section 2, "Restraint and Transport"). Figure 1-1 illustrates a general approach that can be used in all situations.

Once the environment is safe for you and your cat, your next step is to assess the cat's condition quickly, making a mental list of the major problems. Once you have a good idea of the injuries your cat has suffered, you can rank these problems from most to least severe. This two-step process is called **triage** and should always be carried out before any first aid is administered. It assures that you will be concentrating your efforts where they are needed most and increasing the chances of your cat's survival.

When approaching a cat in an emergency, you may see some obvious problems. However, other problems, possibly more life-threatening, may be present. Fortunately, you can quickly evaluate the situation by using a few simple procedures (see Figure 1-1). **First check to see if your cat is responsive.** You can do this by calling the cat's name or stroking his head. If you get no response, *immediately* check the cat's airway, breathing, and circulation. If necessary, start cardiopulmonary resuscitation (see Section 3 and Figure 1-11).

If your cat does respond, the next step is to **take a respiration rate** (breaths per minute; see Figure 1-2). Although normal rates of respiration are 20 to 40 breaths per minute, cats may pant up to 300 breaths per minute. A *decreased respiration rate* may result from *poisoning, hypothermia,* or the late stages of *shock.* An *increased rate* may be caused by *excitement, heat, exercise, pain,* or the early stages of *shock.*

2

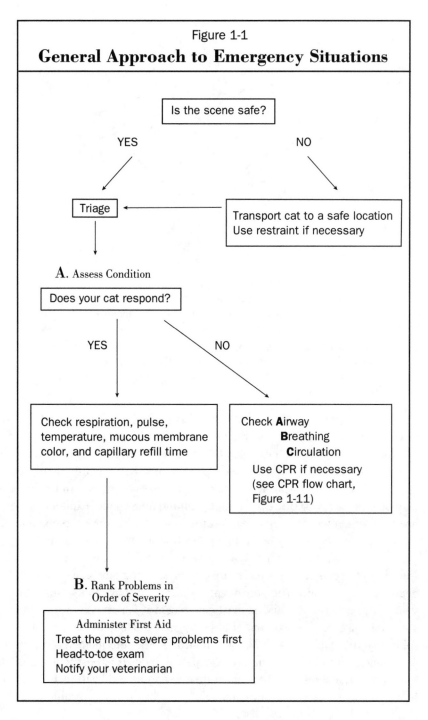

Figure 1-1

Figure 1-1
General Approach to Emergency Situations

Is the scene safe?

YES   NO

Triage ← Transport cat to a safe location
Use restraint if necessary

A. Assess Condition

Does your cat respond?

YES   NO

Check respiration, pulse, temperature, mucous membrane color, and capillary refill time

Check **A**irway
   Breathing
    Circulation
Use CPR if necessary
(see CPR flow chart, Figure 1-11)

B. Rank Problems in Order of Severity

Administer First Aid
Treat the most severe problems first
Head-to-toe exam
Notify your veterinarian

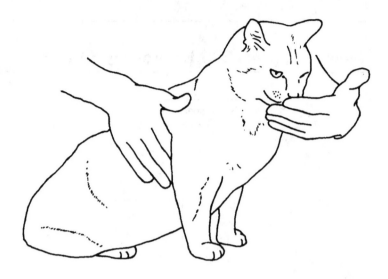

Figure 1-2: To take a cat's respiratory rate, you can either place one hand on the rib cage and feel for the chest moving in and out, or you can place your hand in front of the cat's nostrils, feeling for air movement. Either way, you should count the breaths for 15 seconds and then multiply by 4 to get the number of breaths per minute.

Once you have determined the respiration rate, it is time to **take the pulse** (beats per minute; see Figure 1-3 [left]). If you can't feel a pulse in this location, feel for the heartbeat (see Figure 1-3 [right]). The normal pulse rate is between 100 and 240 beats per minute. Kittens are usually at the upper end. In the late stages of shock and in cases of hypothermia, the pulse may be less than 100 beats per minute. On the other hand, excitement, fever, heart failure, electric shock, snakebite, poisonings, severe pain, and the early stages of shock may result in a pulse that is higher than normal.

Taking a cat's temperature can be very stressful, especially if the cat is sick. If your cat is not extremely stressed or showing any signs of shock (see Section 6), try to **take the temperature.** You will have to use some form of restraint in order to do this, as most cats resent it very much (see Section 2). You can make it less uncomfortable by using a small amount of water-soluble jelly, such as K-Y®, on the tip of the thermometer. Insert the thermometer into the rectum approximately 1 inch. It is best to use a digital thermometer, as these are very accurate and can be read within 1.5 minutes. If you must use a glass thermometer, remember to wait 3 minutes before reading the temperature.

Figure 1-3: Left: To take the cat's pulse rate, place the tips of your fingers along the inside of the cat's thigh, in the groin area, and feel for a pulse. The pulse is taken from a large blood vessel called the femoral artery. Do not press down too hard, or you will not be able to feel the pulse. Count the pulse for 15 seconds and then multiply by 4 to get the beats per minute. **Right:** To feel the heartbeat in a cat, place your hand on the left side of the rib cage, just behind the point of the elbow. Count the beats for 15 seconds and then multiply by 4 to get the beats per minute.

The normal temperature range for a cat is 101°F to 102°F. Temperatures above normal are commonly due to nervousness, heat, exercise, or infection. If a temperature of 1 to 2 degrees above normal persists for more than a few days or is accompanied by other signs (vomiting, diarrhea, convulsions), you should call your veterinarian. Temperatures below normal result mostly from exposure to cold weather for long periods or to severe shock. Temperature extremes and their treatments are discussed in Chapter 3, Section 11.

While you are taking the temperature, you can **check to see if your cat is dehydrated** by using the technique described in Figure 1-4. If you still are not sure whether or not your cat is dehydrated, you can also check to see if the gums are tacky or dry to the touch of your fingertips (see Figure 1-5). Normally, the gums will feel quite wet. *Tackiness indicates dehydration.* Dehydration commonly occurs with shock and prolonged vomiting and diarrhea. Old cats may appear dehydrated when they really are not, because skin elasticity decreases with age. On the other hand, overweight cats may appear to be hydrated even when they really are not, because fat increases skin elasticity. In cases such as these, be sure to check the gums.

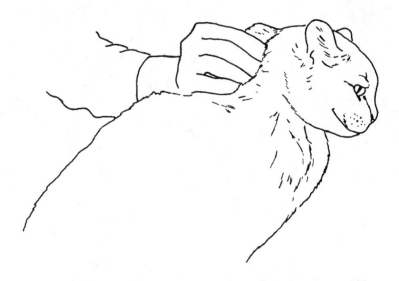

Figure 1-4: To determine if a cat is dehydrated, pick up the skin along the back of your cat's neck with your thumb and forefinger and then let it go. The skin should spring back down immediately if your cat is not dehydrated or very old or thin. The longer it takes to go down, the more dehydrated your cat is.

In addition to taking the pulse, you can use two simple procedures to **check the circulatory system.** One is to look at the color of the gums, and the second is to check the capillary refill time, also via the gums. As shown in Figure 1-5 (left), put your hand on your cat's upper jaw and use your thumb to lift your cat's lip up enough to expose the gums. First examine the color. Normally the gums are pale pink. If they are very pale to white in color, your cat may be in shock or may be anemic due to fleas, ticks, worms, or one of the feline viruses. If the gums are blue, this may indicate shock, heart failure, lung failure, or poisoning. If the gums are brown or blue in color, this may indicate poisoning by acetaminophen (for example, Tylenol®). Red, congested gums may mean your cat either has an abdominal emergency, has been poisoned by carbon monoxide, or has severe heart/lung failure. If the gums are yellow, your cat may have liver failure or may be anemic. If you aren't quite sure of the yellow color, check the color under your cat's tongue, on the roof of the mouth, inside the ear, or in the white of the eye. Check the gums for small red spots. These are pinpoint hemorrhages and are a signal that your cat has a bleeding problem.

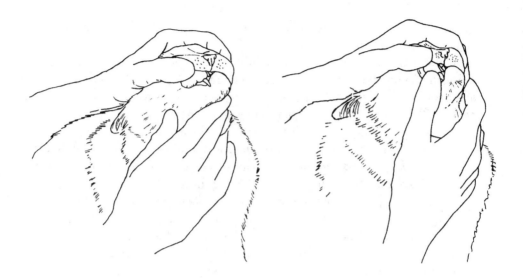

Figure 1-5: Left: To expose your cat's gums, put one hand on the top of the upper jaw, lifting up the lip. Your other hand should cup the lower jaw for restraint. This is a good position to look at the color of the gums, take the capillary refill time, and check the gums for tackiness (dehydration). **Right:** To take the capillary refill time, one hand rests on the upper jaw, with the thumb pulling the lip up. The second hand rests under the lower jaw. Use the thumb of this hand to press firmly on the gums, then immediately remove your thumb. The blanched area should return to a normal pink color within 2 seconds.

After you have had a good look at the color of the gums, take the capillary refill time. This is the time during which the capillaries, the tiny blood vessels just under the gums and skin, will refill once they have been emptied by manual pressure. To do this, see Figure 1-5 (right). A capillary refill time longer than 2 seconds may be due to shock, low heart output, or a blockage in the circulatory system.

Ranking the Problems

After taking the temperature, pulse, and respiration and evaluating the hydration status and circulatory system, you will have a good idea of the general condition of your cat. While each emergency situation will produce a different set of problems, the method for ranking the most life-threatening situations will remain the same.

At the top of the list are situations where your cat is not responsive: no pulse and no breathing or no breathing and a pulse. Both conditions are dire and require knowledge of cardiopulmonary resuscitation techniques (see Section 3). A good example of an emergency that may produce either of these conditions is drowning. When a cat is drowning, the lungs fill up with water and breathing is impossible. *Drowning* is discussed in Section 4 of this chapter. *Choking* is next on the list because your cat will not get a normal amount of oxygen into the lungs. If not helped immediately (see Section 5), the animal could lose consciousness and stop breathing. *Shock and severe bleeding* are listed next. Shock is an insidious condition that accompanies many emergencies. Without intervention, the heart and lungs will stop functioning and your cat will have to be resuscitated. Severe bleeding is a major cause of shock; both are discussed in Section 6.

You may be faced with many other emergencies such as poisonings, burns, and allergic reactions, which may seem just as life-threatening as the conditions discussed above. These emergencies are not discussed here for triage purposes because their ranking is so highly dependent on *each* emergency. For instance, a poisoning may or may not be life-threatening, depending on the poisoning agent, how much was taken, the age of the cat, the time that elapses until first aid is given, other conditions that develop as a result of the poisoning (shock), and so on. These emergencies are discussed in Chapter 3.

The following example illustrates how to use triage in a typical emergency situation:

> You come home to find your cat on your doorstep, seemingly asleep. You call, but your cat does not respond. As you approach your cat, you notice numerous puncture wounds on the sides of his abdomen and chest and a large bleeding laceration on the rump. You evaluate your cat and find there is a pulse but no breathing. In a case such as this, it is important to remember that you must resuscitate your cat before tending to the wounds.
>
> It is tempting to want to take a few minutes to apply a bandage, but in that time, you will lose precious moments that could have been spent trying to resuscitate the cat. However, in a situation where two people are present to help, one would start on resuscitation while the other could quickly apply a bandage and then assist with resuscitation.

In order to respond effectively to an emergency, you should follow the steps listed below before administering first aid:

Assess the environment
- Is it safe?
- Does your cat need restraint?
- Does your cat need to be transported immediately?

Triage—Assess your cat's condition
- Respiration
- Pulse
- Temperature
- Hydration status
- Gum color
- Capillary refill time

Rank the problems from most severe to least severe
- No breathing, no pulse
- No breathing, pulse
- Choking
- Shock/severe bleeding

SECTION 2: RESTRAINT AND TRANSPORT

Sometimes emergencies occur in locations that are too dangerous for you to perform even a quick evaluation of your cat, much less administer first aid. If your cat is hit by a car in the middle of a busy road, your first priority must be to move the cat to a safe location. During the move, restraint is necessary so that you or anyone helping you doesn't get bitten, and proper transport is required so that severe injuries are not exacerbated. This section will explain and illustrate easily applied methods for effective restraint and safe transport.

Restraint

The degree of restraint varies with the type of emergency, the behavior of your cat, and the presence or absence of another person to help. Since cats become stressed very easily, it is important to remain calm and reassure your cat during the entire procedure. You should begin with as little restraint as possible, adding more if necessary. If too much restraint is used initially, your cat may become less willing to cooperate.

Restraining Your Cat

If you have a gentle and cooperative cat and you are by yourself while administering first aid, then you can use the hold shown in Figure 1-6 (left). This will allow you to keep your cat's head and neck in control while using your free hand for first aid. If you are lucky enough to have assistance, then use the hold shown in Figure 1-6 (right).

A cat that has a tendency to jump away or bite can be a challenge to restrain, especially if you are by yourself. If you find yourself in such a situation, use the hold shown in Figure 1-7 (left). Do not be afraid to firmly grasp the skin at the back of the cat's neck. This hold will not hurt your cat! If the skin is not grasped firmly, the hold will not be effective. With assistance, use the hold shown in Figure 1-7 (right).

Figure 1-6: Left: To hold a gentle cat by yourself, place one hand under the cat's lower jaw with your thumb on one side and the rest of your fingers on the other side. Make sure your grip is not so tight that breathing or circulation is restricted. Your other hand is then free to perform first aid or examine your cat. **Right:** If someone is present who can perform first aid while you hold, you can place your cat's front paws between the fingers of your other hand for a more secure hold.

10

Figure 1-7: Left: To hold an uncooperative cat when you are by yourself, grasp the skin firmly at the back of the neck. This leaves your other arm free to examine your cat or give first aid. **Right:** If someone is present who can perform first aid while you hold, place your cat's front paws between the fingers of your other hand for a more secure hold.

Transport

How you choose to transport your cat will largely depend on whether or not there are any broken bones. If your cat has suffered any severe head, neck, back, or leg injuries, such as when hit by a car, then there is a good chance that there will be fractures in the spinal column, pelvis, and/or legs (see Chapter 4, Section 3). In these situations, you must transport your cat properly if you want to avoid causing further injury and pain.

Transporting a Cat with Spinal Cord Injury
Without Assistance: Which method you choose for transport will also depend on what materials you have available and whether or not you have assistance. There are a few methods you can use if you are by yourself and you want to move a cat showing signs of spinal cord damage (paralysis) or possible spinal cord injury related to severe head trauma (unconsciousness; blood or clear fluid from the ear, nose, or mouth; fixed pupils or pupils of different sizes). The method of choice is to use a firm surface, such as a plywood

11

board, heavy cardboard, large serving tray, window screen, or flat sled (see Figure 1-8 [top]). In general, always lay the cat on his side, but if the animal seems uncomfortable in this position, move him onto his chest. It is extremely important not to bend or twist the cat during transport. The second method uses a large towel or blanket (see Figure 1-8 [bottom]).

Figure 1-8: Top: To transport a cat with suspected spinal cord injury, use a plywood board or another firm, flat surface. Gently ease your cat onto the board without twisting or bending the body. Loosely tie your cat to the board with cloth to prevent a fall. **Bottom:** To transport a cat with suspected spinal cord injury when no firm surface is available, ease your cat onto a blanket and gently wrap the blanket around him, taking care not to bend or twist the animal's body. Carry the cat in your arms, keeping the back as straight as possible by supporting the front and hind ends.

With Assistance: If you have assistance, transporting a cat with spinal cord damage is much less difficult than doing it by yourself. The best method is to use a firm surface as described above (see Figure 1-8 [top]). If one is not available, gently ease your cat onto a blanket or large towel and have each person hold a corner of the blanket. Hold the four corners very tightly, to give good support.

With or without help, you should keep the concept of support in mind when transporting a cat with spinal cord injuries in your car. Whether you use a box, carrier, or the backseat of a car, remember to support the cat fully while picking him up and putting him down. If there is no one who can sit in the backseat to keep your cat from moving around as you drive, place pillows or rolled towels on either side of the box, the carrier, or the cat. You should also put some pillows between the front seat and the back seat so that your cat doesn't fall off the seat if you stop suddenly.

Transporting a Cat with Leg or Pelvic Fractures
Cats with leg or pelvic fractures should also be carefully transported. To move a cat showing signs of leg fractures (swelling, limping, too sore to stand), first apply a temporary splint to the broken leg (see Figures 3-2 [bottom], 4-16, and Chapter 4, Section 3). The splint will greatly decrease the swelling that accompanies fractures and make it much easier to repair later. The splint may also allow your cat to stand, if this is the *only* fracture. If your cat can walk with the splint, allow it. If not, he *may* also have a spinal cord injury or other fractures of which you are unaware. In this case, follow one of the methods shown in Figure 1-8, depending on the availability of materials and presence of help.

Keep in mind that if your cat is severely stressed, applying a temporary splint will only stress your cat further; in such a situation, follow one of the methods shown in Figure 1-8. To move a cat showing signs of pelvic fractures (inability to move the back legs, or once standing, the back legs go out sideways), you should follow one of the methods shown in Figure 1-8. If your cat wants to stand, use a towel as a sling (see Figure 4-15 and Chapter 4, Section 3).

Transporting an Ambulatory Cat
All cats, including those that can walk, need to be restrained for safety purposes, during transport in the car as well as from the car to your home, veterinarian's office, or other place. You can use either a pet carrier or a box with several holes in the top. If you have neither a carrier nor a box, then use one of the holds shown in Figures 1-9 or 1-10, depending on whether your cat is cooperative or not.

Figure 1-9: To transport a cooperative cat who is not injured, support the hind end with one arm and wrap your other arm across the front of the cat. The animal should feel secure and be unable to jump out of your arms.

Whatever injury has been sustained, during transport you should keep your cat warm and look for the initial signs of shock: pale gums, restlessness, a rapid, weak pulse and an increased breathing rate. Unfortunately, shock may occur while you are transporting your cat to the hospital. For more on shock, see Section 6.

Summary

In summary, knowledge of proper restraint and transport techniques is of great importance in trying to help a sick or injured cat. With or without assistance, you have a number of effective methods from which to choose, depending upon the circumstances of the injury and the availability of materials.

Figure 1-10: To transport an uncooperative cat who is not injured, support the hind end with one arm and use your other hand to grasp the skin firmly at the back of the neck.

SECTION 3: CPR (Cardiopulminary Resuscitation)

Cardiopulmonary resuscitation is a powerful technique: It provides much needed oxygen to the brain, heart, and other organs during the time when the heart has stopped and your cat cannot breathe on his own. Through your efforts, you may resuscitate him yourself or at least enable a veterinarian to take over and use more advanced CPR techniques to save the cat.

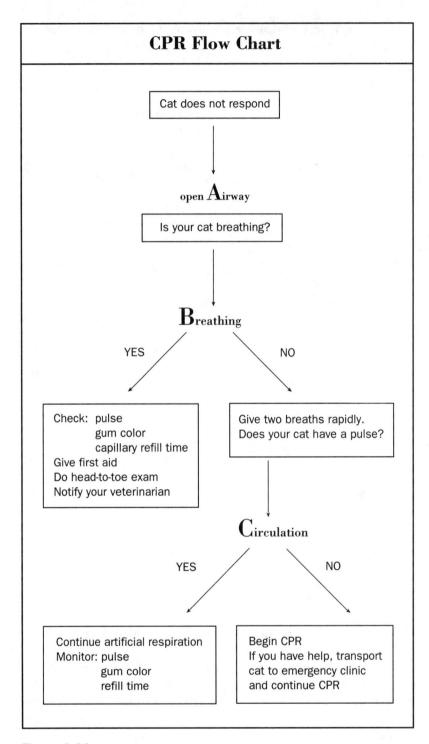

Figure 1-11

As mentioned in the triage section, the first step in assessing your cat's condition is to determine if the animal is responsive to your voice or touch. If the cat does respond, you should evaluate the condition and determine which problem needs to be treated first (see Section 1). However, if your cat does not respond, you may have to resuscitate by beginning CPR *immediately*, as discussed below. If someone is around who can drive, remember that this technique can be used in the car. This would give your cat the best chance of survival, since you have started resuscitation immediately and are on your way to an emergency clinic or veterinary hospital.

The technique of CPR will be discussed by the use of a flow chart (see Figure 1-11) that incorporates the three basic concepts of *airway, breathing, and circulation.* Beginning on the flow chart where your cat is not responsive, the first step must be to *open an airway* (see Figure 1-12).

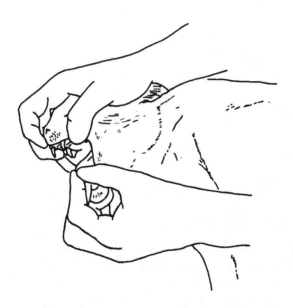

Figure 1-12: To open the airway, first extend the head and neck. Carefully put one hand on the top of the upper jaw to open the mouth and with the middle finger of your other hand, push down on the lower jaw. Use your thumb and index finger to grab the end of the tongue and pull it forward. If you cannot get a good grip on the tongue with your bare fingers, try grabbing the tongue with a cloth. Clear the mouth of all food, vomit, or other obstruction.

Next, *determine if your cat is breathing* (see Figure 1-13). You will be looking at the chest to see if there is any rising or falling, and you will be listening and feeling for air movement against your cheek. If your cat is breathing, you should note the rate. Then take the pulse and temperature, and check the color, refill time, and hydration status (see Section 1). You should notify your veterinarian immediately and continue to monitor the above parameters.

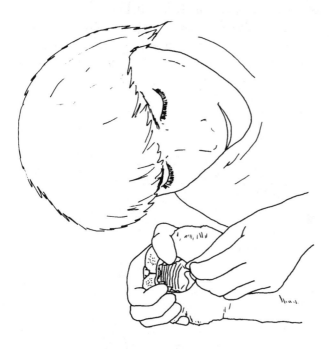

Figure 1-13: To determine if the cat is breathing, hold the head and neck extended and tongue rolled forward. Bend down close to your cat, with your face turned toward his chest and your cheek close to the cat's mouth and nose. Look, listen, and feel for breathing for 10 seconds.

If your cat is not breathing, you must begin artificial respiration (see Figure 1-14). You should see your cat's chest expand. Then take your mouth away so that air can leave the lungs. You may not see the chest expand for three reasons. First, you may not be holding the mouth and lips tightly closed. Second, you may not be blowing with enough force to make the lungs expand. And third, your cat may have an obstruction in the lower airway (see Section 5). Unless you have witnessed your cat choking on an object before becoming unresponsive, you should assume that the chest didn't expand for either of the first two reasons. *Whether you have seen your cat's chest expand or not, next give 2 more breaths quickly.*

Circulation is checked next by *taking your cat's pulse or heartbeat for 10 seconds* (see Figure 1-3). If you find that your cat *does have a pulse,* but is *not breathing,* you must continue artificial respiration at a rate of *20 to 25 times per minute* (1 breath every 3 seconds). Your breaths should be slow and last 1 to 1.5 seconds each. After a minute of artificial respiration, take the pulse for 5 seconds and then look, listen, and feel for 5 seconds to see if breathing has resumed.

If breathing has not resumed, continue artificial respiration, stopping every minute to monitor the pulse and breathing. Sometimes air collects in the stomach and this can be removed by pushing down lightly with the flat of your hand on the left side, just behind the ribs (see Figure 1-15 [top]). You should do this every few minutes or so. If breathing does come back, but is very poor and shallow and your cat is still not responsive, continue artificial respiration at a rate of 10 to 15 times per minute and monitor the pulse every minute.

If you find your cat does not have a pulse and is still not breathing, you must coordinate chest compressions with the artificial respiration. To perform chest compressions, see Figure 1-15 (bottom).

If you are performing CPR by yourself, try to coordinate chest compressions and artificial respiration so that breaths can be given *during* the compressions at a rate of at least 20 times per minute. With a compression rate of 120 times per minute, a breath given with every sixth compression would produce the proper respiration rate.

19

Figure 1-14: To give artificial respiration, have the head and neck extended, the tongue rolled forward and the mouth closed shut by holding both of your hands around your cat's mouth. Place your mouth over your cat's nose and blow air into your cat's nostrils.

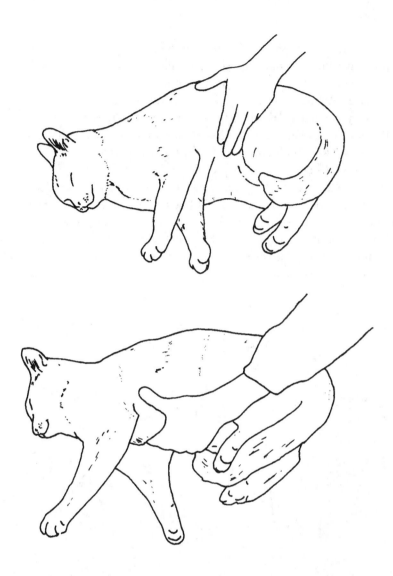

Figure 1-15: Top: To remove air from the stomach, place the flat of your hand on the cat's left side, just behind the ribs, and push down gently. **Bottom:** To compress the chest over the heart from both sides, open your hand around the widest part of the chest and within 1 inch of the point of the elbow so that your thumb is on one side and the rest of your fingers are on the other side. Depress the rib cage 1 to 1.5 inches in a coughlike manner at a rate of 120 to 150 times per minute.

If you are performing CPR with a partner, one person will give artificial respiration while the other person does the chest compressions. The chest compressions should be given at the same rate as if you were by yourself (see above). Artificial respiration should be given during chest compressions with every second or third compression, thus increasing the oxygen flow to the lungs. If you have the assistance of two other people, CPR can be given by two people and the third person can give abdominal compressions between each chest compression (see Figure 1-16). The abdominal compression rate will equal the chest compression rate because they are given alternately. The abdomen should be compressed just as the chest compression is ending so that pressure is maintained on either the chest or abdomen, but never on both at the same time. Abdominal compressions given this way increase the flow of blood to the brain and heart. You should check for a pulse or a heartbeat every 2 minutes during the resuscitation.

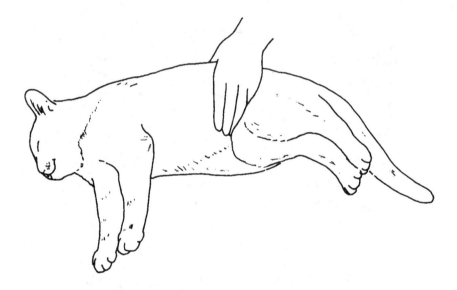

Figure 1-16: To compress the abdomen, press gently with the flat of your hand on the left side at the level of the umbilicus (midabdomen) about 1 inch.

You should continue to give CPR until: (1) a veterinarian can take over, (2) you become exhausted and cannot go on, or (3) you feel a heartbeat or pulse. If a pulse does return, you must continue artificial respiration, as it may take a while before the cat will breathe on his own. If your cat does recover before you can get to a veterinarian, remember to continue to monitor the pulse and respiration until your cat can be thoroughly examined by a veterinarian.

Summary

When faced with an unresponsive cat, remember to check the *ABCs (airway, breathing, and circulation)* and use the appropriate CPR technique for each situation.

PULSE, NO BREATHING

- 20 to 25 breaths/minute (1 breath every 3 seconds)

NO PULSE, NO BREATHING

120 to 150 compressions/minute (2 compressions every 1 second)

- 1 person: 1 breath during every 6th chest compression
- 2 people: 1 breath during every 3rd chest compression
- 3 people: 1 breath during every 3rd chest compression
  (Abdominal compression interposed with chest compression)

SECTION 4: DROWNING

Although most cats are naturally fearful of water, drowning may sometimes happen. Drowning occurs when the lungs fill rapidly with water, making it impossible for a cat to breathe. When coming to the aid of a drowning cat, your first step must be to remove as much water as possible from the lungs.

- Open the airway (see Figure 1-12).
- Next hold your cat upside down by placing your hands around the abdomen, just in front of the hind legs (see Figure 1-17).
- Lay your cat on his side with lowered head and elevated hind-quarters. Check for an open airway again before beginning CPR.
- If your cat does recover from the drowning incident, remember to continue to monitor the pulse and respiration until he can be thoroughly examined by your veterinarian.

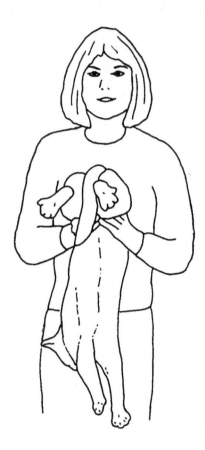

Figure 1-17: To remove water from the lungs, hold the cat upside down by placing your hands around the lower abdomen just in front of the hind legs and gently sway back and forth for 30 seconds.

SECTION 5: CHOKING

Although cats are usually discriminating about what they put in their mouths, there may be times when they try to swallow objects that would be better left alone: food, small toys, tinsel, parts of plants, and other items. Most of the time, your cat will be successful at dislodging the object by a forceful cough. But sometimes, the object becomes stuck and leaves your cat in a choking fit, unable to remove it. If the object is not removed quickly, your cat will not be able to breathe well and may become unconscious. From this point, the cat may stop breathing altogether and need to be resuscitated. This section will explain how to take immediate action to prevent this from happening.

As with CPR, the first aid method for choking can be done in the car. Being able to perform this technique while on the way to the emergency clinic or veterinary hospital will save you precious moments should your cat become unconscious and need to be resuscitated.

Signs of Choking:

- forceful coughing
- eyes bulging
- pawing at mouth

FIRST AID

Conscious Cat
- Open your cat's mouth and look inside (see Figure 1-18). If you can see the object, try to remove it.
- If you cannot see the object, lay your cat on his side with head lowered and hindquarters elevated.
- Place one hand just below the sternum or rib cage and the other hand along the back (see Figure 1-19 [top]). Press in and up.
- You should continue pressing until your cat either coughs up the object or becomes unconscious.

Unconscious Cat
- Lay your cat on his side with head lowered and hindquarters elevated.
- Keep the airway open and tongue pulled out to the side (see Figure 1-12).

25

- Perform two compressions in the same manner as if the cat were conscious (see Figure 1-19 [top]).
- Next check the mouth for foreign objects with a finger sweep (see Figure 1-19 [bottom]).
- Then give two breaths (see Figure 1-14).
- Repeat the cycle of compressions, finger sweep, and artificial respiration until your cat is breathing on his own.
- Every few minutes, check for a pulse.

NOTE: You should not perform the technique shown in Figure 1-19 (top) on a cat with a diagnosed heart or lung abnormality, as the pressure exerted on the chest may exacerbate these conditions. Instead, bring your cat to an emergency clinic immediately.

Figure 1-18: To open your cat's mouth, grasp the upper jaw with the thumb on one side and rest of the fingers on the other side. Gently push down on the front of the lower jaw with the index finger of your other hand.

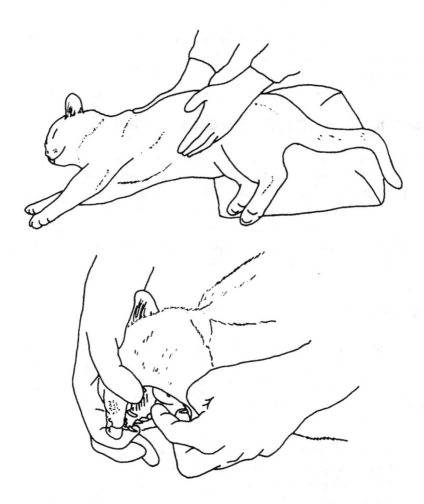

Figure 1-19: Top: Lay your cat on the side with lowered head and elevated hindquarters. Place one hand along the back and the other hand just below the cat's sternum or rib cage, pressing in and up. **Bottom:** To check the mouth for foreign objects, place one hand on the upper jaw, with your thumb on one side and the rest of your fingers on the other side. With your other hand, push down on the lower jaw with your middle finger, keeping your index finger free to sweep back into the mouth.

Summary

The two basic first-aid techniques for a choking cat depend upon whether the cat is conscious or not. Both methods incorporate a Heimlich-like maneuver to remove the object lodged in the airway. For an unconscious cat, two more steps are added: (1) a finger sweep motion to check for a foreign object and (2) artificial respiration to increase the amount of oxygen taken into the lungs.

SECTION 6: SHOCK AND SEVERE BLEEDING

Shock occurs when the circulatory system fails to deliver blood throughout the body. It may be caused by severe bleeding, severe burns, electric shock, prolonged vomiting and diarrhea, allergic reactions (anaphylactic), snake bites, diabetes, or any traumatic injury. Severe blood loss will be discussed in this section; the other causes will be discussed in Chapter 3. Shock requires immediate attention because, if left untreated, *it can rapidly progress to unconsciousness and death.*

Shock

How will you know if your cat is in shock? It may be hard to tell in the very early stages, but as you assess your cat you will note certain problems that, when taken together, mean that shock is beginning:

- increased respiration rate
- increased pulse rate
- gums will appear pale or slightly reddened
- capillary refill time is more than 2 seconds
- general weakness
- restless, anxious behavior

As shock progresses, you will see these signs:

- slow, shallow respiratory rate
- irregular pulse
- gum color is very pale to blue
- capillary refill time is longer than 4 seconds
- pupils become dilated
- very weak to unresponsive to unconscious state
- very cold body temperature (below 98°F)

OBVIOUSLY, IF YOU SEE THE LATE STAGES OF SHOCK, YOUR CAT IS CLOSE TO DEATH.

FIRST AID

- Resuscitate (see CPR, Section 3) and stop severe bleeding.
- Place a blanket or towel under and on top of your cat to prevent loss of body heat.
- Confine your cat.
- Transport your cat immediately to a veterinary clinic (see Section 2 of this chapter). Remember that shock can develop or become worse during transport.
- Do not give your cat anything to drink.
- Do not allow your cat to move around.

Severe Bleeding

Bleeding may be external or internal. If your cat has been hit by a car or has had some other major injury and you see no signs of blood, you *shouldn't* assume there is no bleeding. Because there may be bleeding internally, you should have your cat checked by your veterinarian. If you do notice bleeding, especially large amounts of blood over a short period of time, you should follow the techniques listed below, in the order given, until the bleeding stops. These techniques are more effective when combined and can all be performed in a car.

1. **Direct Pressure:**

   To apply direct pressure, see Figure 1-20. It is better to use a dressing than your bare hand as the cloth will allow a clot to form and can be incorporated into the bandage (see Chapter 4, Section 2). Never remove a pad or cloth that is soaked with blood as you will disturb the clot and bleeding will start again. Instead, place a new pad or cloth on top of the soaked one. The bleeding should stop within 1 to 2 minutes.

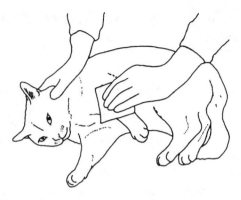

Figure 1-20: To apply direct pressure to a bleeding wound, press down with your bare hand or with a pad.

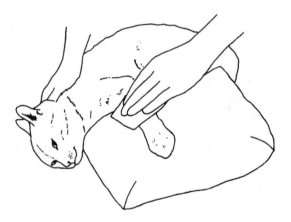

Figure 1-21: Elevate the injured leg above the level of the heart using a pillow, blanket, or towel. This technique can be combined with direct pressure.

2. **Elevate:** Only elevate the injured leg if you are reasonably sure that it is not broken (see Figure 1-21).

3. **Pressure Points:**

If the bleeding is not controlled by direct pressure and elevation, you may also use a pressure point to help stop the bleeding. This is a point where pressure is applied to the main artery supplying the bleeding area. In some cases, you may need help to apply direct pressure and use a pressure point simultaneously. You should be aware of five major pressure points:

- FRONT LEG: For severe bleeding of the front leg, see Figure 1-22.

Figure 1-22: To stop severe bleeding of the front leg, place the flat sides of your fingers on the inside of the upper foreleg about halfway between the shoulder and the elbow. Place your thumb on the outside of the foreleg and press your fingers toward the bone.

- FRONT FOOT: For severe bleeding of the front foot, see Figure 1-23.

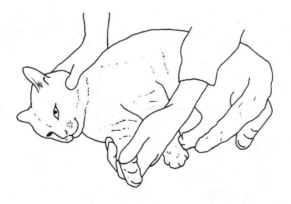

Figure 1-23: To stop severe bleeding on the front paw, place your thumb on the inside of the lower foreleg, just above the cat's foot. Press firmly with your thumb.

- BACK LEG: For severe bleeding of the back leg, see Figure 1-24.

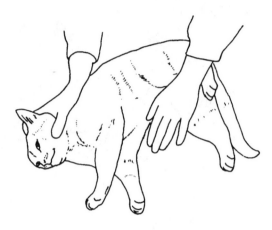

Figure 1-24: To stop severe bleeding of the back leg, press the heel of your hand on the inside of the cat's thigh in the groin area. This is the same place where the pulse is taken.

- BACK FOOT: For severe bleeding of the back foot, see Figure 1-25.

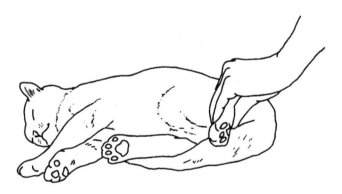

Figure 1-25: To stop severe bleeding of the cat's back foot, place the flat sides of your fingers on the front of the leg, just above the foot. Place your thumb on the back of the leg and press your fingers and thumb together tightly.

- TAIL: For severe bleeding of the tail, see Figure 1-26.

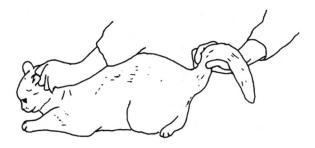

Figure 1-26: To stop severe bleeding of the tail, place your thumb under the middle of the tail and the rest of your fingers around the top of the tail. Press your thumb down tightly.

4. **Pressure Above and Below the Wound:**
   If bleeding is still not controlled, then in addition to the above methods, pressure should be applied directly on the wound and below the wound (see Figure 1-27). If you have help, pressure may also be applied above the wound.

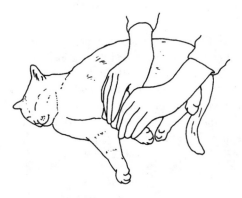

Figure 1-27: To stop severe bleeding that is not controlled by direct pressure, elevation, and pressure points, apply direct pressure *to* the wound itself *and below* the wound. If another person is present, pressure can also be applied above the wound.

5. Tourniquet:

Tourniquets are very dangerous and may easily cause the loss of a limb. The use of a tourniquet should be reserved for situations where bleeding is very severe, all other methods have been tried, and the leg is not expected to be saved. To make a tourniquet, see Figure 1-28. The tourniquet should be left on until a veterinarian can take it off.

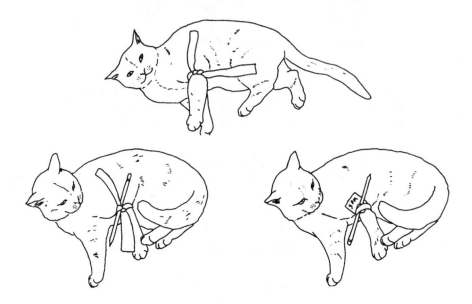

Figure 1-28: Top: To apply a tourniquet, first place a 6- to 12-inch piece of cloth or gauze around the leg just above the bleeding area and tie a knot. **Bottom left:** The second step is to tie a pencil or stick into the knot. **Bottom right:** The third step is to twist the pencil until the bleeding stops and then to tie the pencil down with another piece of cloth so it stays tight. Insert a note bearing the time the tourniquet was applied.

Summary

Knowing how to approach an emergency can save you time in situations where you need to act without hesitation. Understanding the basic first-aid techniques for life-threatening conditions such as cardiopulmonary arrest, shock, drowning, and choking will enable you to help your cat *immediately* and greatly increase his chances of survival.

What to Do Second:
The Head-to-Toe Exam

O nce you have performed basic life-saving techniques and your cat's condition is stable, take a closer look at your cat to make sure there are no other problems. For example, a cat who has been hit by a car may have severe internal injuries that you can't see but might be able to detect on examination. Once you understand how to check your cat and know what to look for, you can do a head-to-toe exam in 5 to 10 minutes, identify other problems your cat might have, and then give the appropriate first aid. Like the basic life-saving techniques, the physical exam can be performed in a car on the way to the emergency clinic or veterinary hospital. During the exam, it is important to be as calm and gentle as possible in order to minimize stress.

In this chapter, you will learn how to examine the major body systems quickly. The common emergencies for each system will be described and first aid measures will be detailed. In all cases, *be sure to contact your veterinarian* if you have access to a telephone to determine if your cat should be seen immediately. Many of the first-aid methods in the following sections involve bandages. The reader will be referred to the bandaging section (Chapter 4, Section 2) in these instances. Many bandages, especially those applied to the head or the extremities, will stay on better and longer if your cat wears an Elizabethan collar. These collars are discussed in the bandaging section. Before you begin the head-to-toe exam, take the temperature,

Normal

Protruded

Dilated   **Constricted**

Normal

Figure 2-1: The third eyelid: Top: normal. **Middle:** protruded. **Bottom:** Pupil size in room light.

pulse, and respiratory rate (see Chapter 1, Section 1, "Triage") if you have not already done so.

SECTION 1: EYES

To start the *exam,* find out if your cat can see. A cat with impaired vision may walk tentatively around walls or refuse to move at all. Unfamiliar surroundings may cause your cat to hesitate and smell along before walking. Next, look at the eyes. If only one eye is injured, compare the injured eye to the normal eye.

Check the following: position of the third eyelid (see Figure 2-1, [top]), change in the color of the iris, pupil size (see Figure 2-1, [bottom]), response to light, eyeball position, squinting, and excessive blinking or tearing. In a normal cat, the third eyelids are not noticeable, but under certain circumstances may protrude over the surface of the eyeball. To check the pupil size, shine a flashlight into your cat's eye (checking one eye at a time). The pupil should become smaller (constrict). When you remove the light, the pupil should return to the original size. If you bring your cat into a dimly lighted room, the pupil should become larger (dilate). When you shine the flashlight into the eye, you should also note your cat's behavioral response to the light. If she turns away, squints, or starts blinking or tearing, her eye may be painful. You can check the position of the eyeball from the front and the side. The eyeball should be neither sunken in nor pushed out. Your cat's eyes should be clear with no noticeable discharge. If you do see a discharge, note the color and consistency (for example, yellow and thick).

Glaucoma

Glaucoma occurs when the pressure within the eye increases. The signs of this disease are:

- Squinting
- Dilated pupil
- Pupil that slowly constricts or does not constrict at all
- Turning away from the light
- Tearing
- Steamy appearance to the eye
- Enlarged eyeball (seen late in the course of the disease)

Although there is no first aid as such, it is important to be able to quickly recognize the signs of this disease and have your cat examined immediately, as permanent damage to the eye can occur in a few days.

Prolapse of the Eye

The eyeball is prolapsed when it is partially or fully out of the socket. It usually occurs in conjunction with a fight, fall, or being hit by a car.

FIRST AID

- Cover the eye with a sterile pad or cloth that has been moistened in cold sterile saline or cold water.
- Bandage the eye to the socket area by loosely wrapping with gauze and adhesive (see Chapter 4 and Figure 4-5).
- Do not attempt to push the eye back into the socket. Have your cat seen as soon as possible.

Foreign Object in the Eye

A stone, piece of glass, BB pellet, sand, or similar small object may become lodged in your cat's eye. Look carefully to see if the object has penetrated the eye. The signs of this condition are:

1. Presence of a foreign object in the eye
2. Blinking
3. Squinting
4. Tearing
5. Turning away from the light

FIRST AID

- Lift the upper eyelid and look very carefully for the foreign object. If the eye is clear, relax the skin of the upper eyelid and pull down gently on the skin of the lower eyelid using the thumb of the other hand. Again, look carefully for the object (see Figure 2-2 [top left and right]).

For a nonpenetrating object
- Wash it out by gently pouring sterile saline or cool water onto the eye surface for a few minutes (see Figure 2-2 [bottom left]).
- Another method is to ease the foreign object carefully out of the eye by using a cotton swab moistened with cool, fresh water (see Figure 2-2 [bottom right]).
- If you cannot remove the object from the eye, place a sterile pad or cloth over the eye and bandage as shown in Figure 4-5 in Chapter 4, Section 2. The bandage will prevent your cat from scratching or rubbing the eye and causing further injury.

For a penetrating object
- Do not attempt to remove the object.
- To prevent further trauma, put an Elizabethan collar on your cat (see Figure 4-13 in Chapter 4, Section 2) until she can be examined by your veterinarian.

Trauma to the Eye Surface

The surface of the eye (cornea) may become irritated by scratches from other cats, chemical burns, or the presence of foreign objects in the eye (see discussion above). You might suspect the cornea has been irritated if the eye appears normal except for the following signs:

1. Blinking
2. Squinting
3. Redness
4. Tearing
5. Turning away from the light

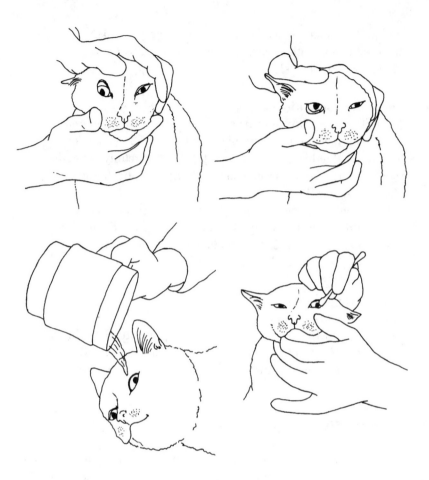

Figure 2-2: Top left: To look for an object in the upper surface of the cat's eye, place one hand directly above the eye while the other hand holds the lower jaw. With the hand above the eye, pull gently up on the skin. **Top right:** To check the lower surface of the eye, relax the skin above the eye and use the thumb of your hand on the lower jaw to pull down the skin just below the eye. **Bottom left:** To wash a foreign object out of the eye, gently pour cool water or sterile saline onto the eye surface for a few minutes. **Bottom right:** To remove a foreign object from the eye with a cotton swab, first moisten the swab with cool water or sterile saline. Hold the swab in one hand, carefully easing the foreign object out of the eye with the tip of the swab, while the other hand holds the lower jaw for restraint.

FIRST AID

Scratches
- To rest the eye and prevent further injury, cover the eye with a sterile pad or clean cloth.
- Bandage loosely to the head, leaving the normal eye unbandaged (see Figure 4-5 in Chapter 4, Section 2).

Chemical Burns
- The chemical should be washed out immediately.
- Pour plenty of cool water onto the eye surface for at least 5 minutes (see Figure 2-2 [bottom left]).
- To rest the eye and prevent further injury, cover the injured eye with a sterile pad or clean cloth and bandage loosely to the head, leaving the normal eye free (see Figure 4-5 in Chapter 4, Section 2).

> NOTE: Have your veterinarian perform a complete eye exam on your cat as soon as possible to determine the extent of injury to the cornea.

Trauma to the Lids

The eyelids may become traumatized during any severe injury, for example, being hit by a car or being involved in a fight with another animal. The lids will appear:

1. Torn
2. Bruised
3. Swollen

FIRST AID

- Hold a cold compress (not ice) over the lid for 5 to 10 minutes to reduce swelling.
- Cover with a clean, dry pad and bandage loosely to the head, leaving the unaffected eye unbandaged (see Figure 4-5 in Chapter 4, Section 2).

41

Blood in the Eye

Severe head trauma or penetrating eye wounds may cause blood in the eye. It may clear on its own in seven to fourteen days without any further problems or it may be complicated by glaucoma or retinal detachment.

FIRST AID

- Since movement may increase the bleeding, keep your cat as quiet and confined as possible until she can be examined.

SECTION 2: EARS

To examine the ears, first determine if your cat can hear. Stand behind your cat, rattle some stones in a food dish or call your cat and look for a response. Since the mechanism that controls the sense of balance is located in the ear, you should closely observe the way the cat walks. A cat whose balance is off will hesitate to walk and may have a noticeable head tilt (see Vestibular Syndrome, Chapter 3, Section 14). Be sure also to examine both the outside and inside of the ear for the following: bite wounds, discharge, swellings, plant materials, and ticks.

Hematoma

A **hematoma** is a swelling that contains blood. It is usually caused by violent head shaking or scratching, or it develops from a bite wound. The major sign is a soft, fluctuant swelling on the ear.

FIRST AID

- If your cat cannot be examined by your veterinarian immediately, bandage the affected ear (see Figure 4-6 in Chapter 4, Section 2) to prevent the hematoma from enlarging.

Foreign Objects

Foreign objects such as plant material and ticks may become embedded in the ear canal. Depending upon how far into the ear canal the foreign object has gone, your cat may have some or all of the following signs:

1. Head shaking
2. Rotating the head with the affected ear down
3. Falling and circling to the affected side
4. Inability to eat and drink normally
5. Fever

FIRST AID

- If the foreign object is visible and your cat will stay still, remove the object with tweezers or your fingers and save it for identification (see Figure 2-3).
- If you suspect a foreign object in the ear, bandage the ear (see Figure 4-6 in Chapter 4, Section 2) until your cat can be examined. This will prevent further injury to the ear, including hematoma formation.

Lacerations

Your cat's ear may become lacerated or torn from fighting with another animal. The major sign will be a very bloody ear.

FIRST AID

- Stop the bleeding by direct pressure (see Chapter 1, Section 6).
- Leave the cloth on the clot and bandage the ear (see Figure 4-6 in Chapter 4, Section 2).

Vestibular Syndrome

This emergency will be discussed in Chapter 3, Section 14.

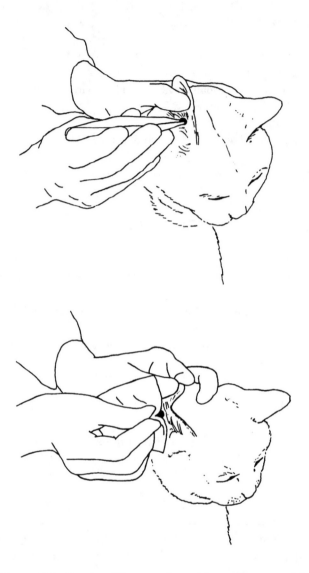

Figure 2-3: Foreign objects, such as ticks or plant material, may be removed from your cat's ear with either tweezers or your fingers: **Top:** To remove a foreign object with tweezers, grasp the object with the tweezers about the part that is closest to the skin of the ear and pull out evenly. **Bottom:** To remove a foreign object with your fingers, cradle the object with your thumb and first two fingers where it is closest to the skin and pull straight out. If the foreign object is a tick, use a tissue or cloth when pulling to avoid exposing yourself to the tick.

SECTION 3: NOSE

To *examine* the nose and nasal passageways, observe the breathing and shine a flashlight into the nostrils. Normal breathing is in and out through the nose at 20 to 40 breaths per minute. Your cat should not be panting unless the environment is hot or stressful. When you shine a flashlight into the nostrils, look for any deformity, obstructions, or discharge. If discharge is present, note the type (blood, pus, water) and if it is coming from one or both nostrils. The nose itself *may or may not* be moist.

Nosebleed

Blood coming from one or both nostrils is usually caused by a traumatic injury, but may also be caused by a foreign object, tumor in the nasal passages, bleeding disorder, or repeated sneezing.

FIRST AID

- Keep your cat quiet and confined.
- Apply cold compresses to the nose. Do *not* use ice—it may cause freezing.
- Do not tilt the head back to lessen the bleeding, as your cat may choke on the blood.
- Do not pack the nostrils with gauze, as this may cause sneezing and more bleeding.

Foreign Objects

These usually consist of plant material that has lodged in the nasal passageways. The signs you may see are:

1. Frequent episodes of sneezing or snorting
2. Banging of the head
3. Blood from the nose

FIRST AID

- If you can see a foreign object, try to remove it with tweezers (see Figure 2-4).

45

- If you cannot remove the foreign object or don't see one, have your cat examined by your veterinarian.
- Treat the nosebleed as described above.

Figure 2-4: To remove a foreign object from the nose, steady the cat's head with one hand and use the tweezers with your other hand.

SECTION 4: MOUTH/THROAT

To examine the mouth and throat, first open the mouth fully (see Figure 1-18). You will get a much better view if you open your cat's mouth under a bright lamp or have a friend hold a flashlight as you look. Note the smell of the mouth: a very foul odor may indicate infection somewhere in the mouth; a very sweet smell may indicate a disease state, for example, diabetes.

Next, check the gums, the teeth, and the tongue. The gum color should be pale pink and the capillary refill time should be less than 2 seconds (see Chapter 1, Section 1). Note any chipped, broken, or decayed teeth. Check under the tongue for foreign objects such as string or tinsel and note the presence of tumors here or anywhere else in the mouth. Finally, observe your cat chewing and swallowing food. You might suspect a painful mouth if the cat drools excessively, paws at her mouth, or appears hungry but avoids food and water. Under the same circumstances, she might extend her neck or choke as she tries to swallow.

Foreign Objects

Some cats, especially kittens, may be unable to resist eating certain objects, such as a long piece of string, thread, dental floss, or a shiny piece of tinsel. Depending on how far down in the throat the foreign object gets, you may see signs of:

1. Drooling
2. Blood from the mouth
3. Neck extension on swallowing
4. Choking while swallowing
5. Appetite, but not eating or drinking
6. Vomiting

FIRST AID: STRING OR STRINGLIKE FOREIGN OBJECT

- Open your cat's mouth as shown in Figure 1-18 and look under the tongue.
- Check to see if any part of the string has been swallowed.
- If part has been swallowed, do not pull the remaining piece, as you may cause severe damage. It must be removed by your veterinarian.
- If the string is loose in the mouth, remove it slowly and carefully. If you feel resistance, stop pulling and have your cat examined by your veterinarian.

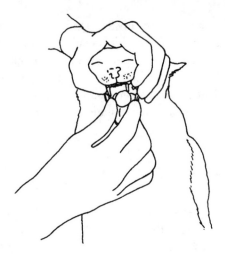

Figure 2-5: To remove a foreign object from your cat's mouth, place one hand on the upper jaw, with the thumb on one side and the rest of the fingers on the other side. Use the middle finger of your other hand to gently open the lower jaw. This technique leaves your thumb and index finger free to either remove a foreign object directly or use a tweezers to do so.

FIRST AID: OTHER FOREIGN OBJECTS

- If you can see the foreign object, remove it carefully with your hand or tweezers (see Figure 2-5).
- If the foreign object is not right at the front of the mouth but can be seen further back, have a friend hold your cat's mouth open while you try to remove the foreign object.
- If you cannot see a foreign object but your cat is choking, treat the choking as discussed in Chapter 1, Section 5.

Mouth Burns

The mouth of your cat may become burned by chewing on an electric cord or by contact with a caustic chemical or hot liquid. Signs of mouth burns are:

1. Drooling
2. Avoidance of food and water

3. Avoidance of petting around the mouth and face
4. Pawing at the mouth
5. Burns in and around the mouth

FIRST AID

- If the mouth burn is due to chewing on an electric cord, see Chapter 3, Section 8, "Electric Shock."
- If the mouth burn is due to contact with a chemical or hot liquid, lay your cat on her side, neck and body resting on a pillow, with head lower than the rest of her body. Lift up the lip to expose the teeth and flush large amounts of cool water through the mouth by using a cup or a slowly running hose (see Figure 2-6).

> NOTE: You should *not* rinse your cat's mouth if she is not fully awake or becomes too stressed. Under these conditions, *see your veterinarian immediately.*

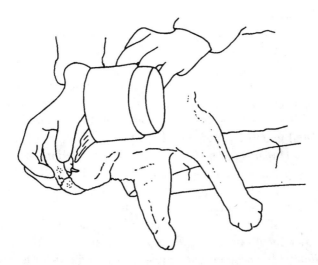

Figure 2-6: To rinse your cat's mouth, first place a pillow or rolled towel under the neck and shoulders so that the head is lowered. With one hand, lift up your cat's lip toward the back of the mouth. The other hand holds a cup or a *slowly* running hose. Flush large amounts of cool water through the mouth.

Blood from the Mouth

This emergency is usually due to a severe trauma of some sort, usually an auto accident or a fight. The blood may be coming from a wound in the mouth (such as a broken tooth) or may be due to internal bleeding or a severe head injury.

FIRST AID

- Use a flashlight and try to find where the blood is coming from. Check the teeth.
- If you can see the wound in the mouth, apply a cold compress directly on it with pressure until the bleeding stops. This may be difficult, depending on the location of the wound.
- *If you do not see a source of the blood, notify your veterinarian* because your cat should be examined immediately.
- Look for signs of shock (Chapter 1, Section 6). Monitor gum color, refill time, and pulse.
- Do not tilt the head back to stop the bleeding, as your cat may choke on the blood.

SECTION 5: CHEST

To examine the chest, check the following: chest wall symmetry, breathing, and pain or wounds on the chest. To look at the symmetry of the chest wall, stand behind your cat. As she breathes, you should see both sides of the chest rise and fall equally. Listen closely to the breathing. The rate varies between 20 and 40 breaths per minute (see Chapter 1, Section 1). Is your cat having difficulty breathing at rest or during play? Difficult breathing is heavy, may be noisy, and may be at a faster rate than normal. If your cat is not getting enough oxygen through the nose, then she will start breathing through the mouth. If the breathing difficulty begins suddenly and rapidly progresses to open-mouth breathing, *have your cat examined by your veterinarian immediately.* To check for pain, press *gently* on the ribs with your fingers. A cat in pain may scratch, bite, or try to move away. Finally, use your fingertips to feel along the fur over the chest for dried blood or puncture wounds.

Feline Asthma

This emergency is discussed in Chapter 3 (Typical Emergencies), Section 2.

Upper Airway Obstructions

The upper airways (trachea, bronchi) may become blocked if your cat accidentally inhales something she is trying to eat, for example, parts of a plant such as pine needles. The major signs associated with this problem are:

1. Labored breathing on inhalation
2. Wheezing or high-pitched sound on inhalation
3. May or may not have a cough

There is no specific first aid except to keep your cat calm and confined until examined by your veterinarian.

Rib Fractures

The ribs may become fractured in any case of chest trauma. You will see the following signs:

1. Unsymmetrical chest wall (the side that doesn't rise as much may have a fractured rib)
2. Painful breathing
3. Pain when the rib is pressed
4. Possible wound

FIRST AID

- Keep your cat quiet and confined.
- Lay your cat on her side with the fractured rib down. In this way, the fractured rib will exert no pressure on the lung that will be ventilated the most (the top one). If your cat resists this position, let her assume the position that is most comfortable for her.

Chest Wounds

Chest wounds occur with any severe trauma to the chest wall. The wounds may create an opening all the way into the chest cavity or stay outside the chest cavity. The signs seen with chest wounds are:

1. Difficulty breathing
2. Muscles of the chest wall may be exposed
3. Possible fractured ribs
4. Possibly the sound of air being sucked in and out of the chest cavity

FIRST AID

- If the skin is broken, do not wash or clean.
- Soak a pad or cloth in sterile saline or cool water and place the pad over the wound immediately after your cat breathes out.
- Bandage firmly (see Figure 4-8 in Chapter 4, Section 2).
- Make sure your cat is not breathing with more difficulty once the bandage is in place. Rebandage if necessary.
- Maintain an open airway if necessary.
- Monitor breathing until your cat can be examined.

SECTION 6: ABDOMEN

To examine a cat's abdominal area, look at the symmetry of the abdomen and also feel for pain and wounds. Stand behind your cat and look at both sides of the abdomen; they should be about the same size. Press your hands gently down on the abdomen. A cat with a painful abdomen will hold her belly in a tight, tense fashion. Alternatively, she may want to lie down on a cool surface. To check for dried blood and wounds, place your fingertips on the middle of your cat's belly. Move them slowly over the skin and fur until you have covered the entire abdomen. Be sure to check the litterbox if you suspect your cat may be behaving abnormally or acting sick. A litterbox that hasn't been used in more than 24 hours may be a sign of trouble. Try to observe your cat in the box. A cat who is straining in the box may be constipated or may have a urinary tract blockage (see Chapter 3, Section 13). Both conditions should be reported to your veterinarian immediately. Finally, check the vulva or penis for abnormal discharge or unusual odor: both may be signs of infection and should also be reported to your veterinarian.

Gastric Foreign Objects

If your cat happens to swallow a small toy, needle, pin, or piece of string, it may cause an obstruction or puncture internal organs if not removed. You may see the following signs:

1. Tightened abdominal muscles
2. Vomiting
3. Rapid pulse
4. Loss of appetite
5. Fever
6. Abdominal distention (with an obstruction only)
7. Reduced production of feces (with an obstruction only)

There is no first aid for a gastric foreign object except to recognize the signs and to have your cat examined by your veterinarian *as soon as possible.*

Nonpenetrating Injuries

Injuries to the abdomen when the skin is not broken are caused mostly by automobile accidents and include the rupture or bruising of abdominal organs. Generally, the signs seen are the same as with gastric foreign bodies (without an obstruction) but will vary depending on which organ is ruptured or bruised:

1. Bloody urine or no urine (damage to the urinary tract)
2. Pain over the part of the abdomen closest to the head (spleen or liver damage)

There is no first aid as such for nonpenetrating injuries. However, if you suspect this condition, you should have your cat examined immediately by your veterinarian.

Penetrating Injuries

Arrows, knives, and gunshot are the common causes of penetrating injuries of the abdomen. The signs you may see are:

1. Rapid pulse
2. Rapid breathing
3. Severe abdominal pain
4. Protruding abdominal organs
5. Shock

FIRST AID

- Treat shock (see Chapter 1, Section 6) *on the way to your veterinarian.*
- If there are protruding abdominal organs, place a clean cloth that has been moistened with sterile saline or cool water around the protruding organs and wrap these against the abdomen and bandage (see Figure 4-8 in Chapter 4, Section 2). *Do not* try to push the protruding organs back into the abdomen and do not wash the wound.
- If a knife is penetrating the abdomen, it can be pulled out. Once you have pulled the knife out, apply a pad over the wound and bandage (see Figure 4-8 in Chapter 4, Section 2). Do not wash first.
- *Do not* remove any sharp objects that may cause more damage upon removal (for example, arrows). Simply bandage around this area without washing as you would for a knife wound.

Sudden Stomach Upset (Gastritis)

Your cat may get gastritis when she eats garbage, spoiled food, or table scraps. The signs include:

1. Vomiting
2. Diarrhea (sometimes with blood)
3. Dehydration
4. Pain in the upper abdomen

- If your cat appears dehydrated (see Figure 1-4 and 1-5 [top]), *see your veterinarian immediately.*
- If your cat is not dehydrated and is vomiting, withhold food and water for 12 to 24 hours and then offer small amounts.
- If your cat is not dehydrated and has diarrhea but no vomiting, withhold food for 12 to 24 hours and restrict water to small amounts offered often. At the end of the 12 to 24 hours, offer small amounts of food along with the water.
- If the vomiting/diarrhea persists during the 12 to 24 hours or begins again upon feeding, have your cat examined by your veterinarian.

> **NOTE: Never withhold water from a cat who has impaired kidney function; instead, see your veterinarian immediately. For more information on vomiting/diarrhea, see Chapter 3, Section 15.**

Rectal Prolapse

The rectum may prolapse in cats that strain due to constipation, urinary tract obstruction, tumors, or giving birth. The signs seen are:

1. Round mass of tissue protruding from the anus
2. Color of the tissue is initially red, turning dark red later

FIRST AID

- Wrap a clean cloth that has been moistened with cool water around the cylindrical mass. This will keep the tissue moist until it can be manipulated to its normal position by your veterinarian.

SECTION 7: EXTREMITIES

Trauma from automobile accidents and fights with other animals may cause both your cat's front and hind legs to be badly injured. To examine the legs, you should watch your cat walk, look at the joints, and check for the presence of pain, wounds, or broken bones. As you watch, look to see if your cat favors one leg over the others. The joints should not be swollen or puffy. To check for pain, press with your fingertips all along the leg. Lightly pinch the toes to see if she pulls the leg away. This means that the cat can feel the pain. Finally, use a comb or your fingertips to run through the fur looking for dried blood, torn skin, or other evidence of wounds.

Fractures

The bones in the legs may break when trauma is severe, such as from auto accidents or falls from high places. If your cat is favoring one leg, there may be a fracture. For a more complete discussion on the topic of fractures, see Chapter 4, Section 3.

FIRST AID

- If you suspect a fracture, splint the leg before moving your cat (see Chapter 4, Section 3).

Wounds

The skin, muscles, nerves, and blood vessels may become torn or punctured due to bites or a severe trauma, such as an auto accident. Wounds may accompany fractures. If wounds are not cleaned out quickly, infection may develop, causing pain and lameness. Bite or claw wounds often seal over quickly and produce abscesses. For a more complete discussion on the topic of wounds, see Chapter 4, Section 1.

FIRST AID

- For wounds that are bleeding heavily, first stop the bleeding (see Chapter 1, Section 6) and then bandage (see Chapter 4, Section 2).
- For superficial wounds, clean the wound and then apply a bandage (see Chapter 4, Sections 1 and 2).

NOTE: If your cat has been in an auto accident or fallen from a high place, check her thoroughly, as there may be severe trauma to other parts of the body.

56

Table 2-1: Head-to-Toe Exam

Body Part	Checkpoints
EYES	sight position of third eyelid change in color of the iris pupil size response to light eyeball position squinting excessive blinking or tearing
EARS	hearing balance bite wounds discharge swellings plant materials ticks
NOSE	breathing deformity obstructions discharge
MOUTH, THROAT	smell gums teeth tongue chewing swallowing
CHEST	chest wall symmetry breathing pain wounds
ABDOMEN	abdominal symmetry pain wounds
LEGS	walking joints pain wounds abscesses
MENTAL STATE	alert depressed drowsy hyperexcited disoriented

SECTION 8: RESPONSIVENESS

If your cat is behaving differently than usual, this may be a clue that something is wrong, even if you found no problems during the rest of the head-to-toe exam. Make a quick note to examine your cat's responsiveness. Check to see if she is alert, depressed, drowsy, hyperexcited, or disoriented. A sudden behavior change may be a prelude to severe changes in the nervous system, as seen with seizures or coma. *Have the cat examined by your veterinarian* to determine a cause. Both seizures and coma are discussed in Chapter 3.

SUMMARY

The head-to-toe exam is a crucial component of first aid. Performed only when your cat is stabilized, it can alert you to problems that may become serious in a short time. Table 2-1 contains a list of points to check in each body system.

3

Typical Emergencies and How to Handle Them

T he emergencies discussed in this chapter all have one common characteristic: if left untreated, they have the potential to cause life-threatening problems quickly. Because they can cause such serious problems, recognizing the signs of these conditions and acting quickly is very important. If you have access to a phone during the emergency, call your veterinarian for advice. This is an important part of first aid for all emergencies listed in this chapter. Your veterinarian can tell you whether to bring your cat into the clinic right away or if you can continue to provide care at home.

SECTION 1: ALLERGIC REACTIONS

Two types of allergic reactions that require emergency care are anaphylactic shock and hives. Both are immediate hypersensitivity reactions and fortunately both are rare in cats.

Anaphylactic Shock

Anaphylactic shock may be caused by a number of different agents, including antibiotic and local anesthetic drugs, hormones, vaccines, insect bites, and food. In a sensitive cat, these substances produce within minutes a reaction that may cause both the circulatory and respiratory systems to fail. The signs are:

1. Difficulty breathing
2. Vomiting
3. Diarrhea
4. Head scratching
5. Incoordination
6. Shock

FIRST AID

- Open the airway (see Figure 1-12).
- Perform CPR, if necessary (see Chapter 1, Section 3).
- Treat for shock on the way to your veterinarian (see Chapter 1, Section 6).

Hives

Hives may be caused by insect bites or injections of vaccines or drugs. The signs are localized to the head and may be seen from 20 minutes to 2 hours after the bite or injection:

1. Redness, swelling in the eyes and mouth
2. Intense itching of the swollen areas
3. Rubbing face on the ground
4. Head scratching
5. Difficulty breathing

FIRST AID

- If the reaction is severe and your cat is having difficulty breathing, notify your veterinarian at once and monitor breathing.
- Put an Elizabethan collar on your cat if he has inflicted rubbing and scratching wounds to his head (see Chapter 4, Section 2 and Figure 4-13).
- Treat the wounds on the face (for general treatment of wounds, see Chapter 4, Section 1).

SECTION 2: ASTHMA

Asthma, when it occurs suddenly, is considered to be life-threatening. During an attack, the air passages become so narrowed that the amount of air passing to and from the lungs is severely restricted. A cause for asthma has not been found, although many believe it to be allergy related. Some substances that may trigger asthmatic attacks in cats are litter dust, cigarette smoke, flea spray, aerosol sprays in general, and feather pillows. The signs are:

1. Difficulty breathing
2. May be coughing
3. May be wheezing
4. Cyanosis
5. May have prolonged, forced exhalations

FIRST AID

- *Do not stress the cat! Your cat may die from being stressed during an asthmatic attack.*
- If your cat is having difficulty breathing, *call your veterinarian* and have your cat seen immediately.
- *Provide CPR* support as needed (see Chapter 1, Section 3).

> NOTE: In trying to determine a cause, think of anything that changed recently that might have preceded these signs, for example, changing to scented litter, a different perfume, a different floor/rug cleaner, and so on.

SECTION 3: BIRTHING PROBLEMS

Birthing difficulties may be caused by a small birth canal, weak uterine contractions, or an abnormal fetus. Once the kittens are born, they may have difficulty breathing if the mother doesn't lick open the membrane sac. If you can recognize the signs that indicate these problems, you can increase the chances that your cat will recover quickly and the kittens will be healthy.

Keep in mind that a cat may deliver normal, healthy kittens one to three days apart. The signs of birthing problems are:

1. Gestation (the length of the pregnancy) shorter than 56 days or longer than 70 days
2. Sixty minutes of strong abdominal contractions without the birth of a kitten
3. Pain or any sign of illness
4. Black, yellow, or bloody vaginal discharge is present. (Note: A greenish-black discharge indicates placental separation, and a kitten should be born within 1 to 2 hours.)
5. Kittens not breathing immediately after birth.

FIRST AID

For the mother:
- If you see any signs of birthing problems or if your cat has had any previous birthing problems, call your veterinarian.

For the kittens:
- Open the membrane sac if the mother hasn't done so.
- If the kitten does not start breathing immediately, follow the procedures below in the order given:

   (a) Use a moistened cotton swab to remove mucus from the mouth and nostrils.
   (b) Cup the kitten in your hands with the head downward and gently swing to remove more mucus from the nasal passages.
   (c) Vigorously rub the kitten all over for a minute.
   (d) Start CPR.

SECTION 4: BITES AND STINGS

This section will cover bites, stings, and poisonings from many different types of animals: cats, dogs, and wild animals such as raccoons, snakes, ticks, flying insects, spiders, scorpions, and lizards.

Domestic/Wild Animal Bites

Bites by domestic or wild animals will cause the following signs:

1. Skin is punctured or torn by teeth.
2. Area is red and swollen.
3. Bleeding will be slight or extensive.

If your cat is not vaccinated for rabies and is bitten by a rabid animal, he may also show signs of:

1. Sudden change in behavior (some cats, especially kittens, become very affectionate before they become vicious)
2. Restlessness
3. Viciousness
4. Convulsions
5. Drooling
6. Paralysis

FIRST AID

- Control bleeding (see Chapter 1, Section 6).
- Wash wound with soap and water (see Figure 3-1 [Top] and Chapter 4, Section 1). Wear gloves if you suspect your cat was bitten by a rabid animal.
- Apply a loose bandage (see Figure 3-1 [bottom] and Chapter 4, Section 2).
- If you think your cat may have been bitten by a rabid animal, call your health authority immediately.
- If your cat was exposed to a rabid animal and the rabies vaccination is up to date, your cat should be boostered with *another rabies shot.*
- If your cat was exposed to a rabid animal and the rabies vaccination is not up to date, your cat will have to undergo a quarantine at your expense.

Snakebite

Probably because of a cautious, wise demeanor, the cat is less often a victim of a snakebite than the dog. And when bitten, the cat will often survive a bite that would have been fatal to a dog of the same size.

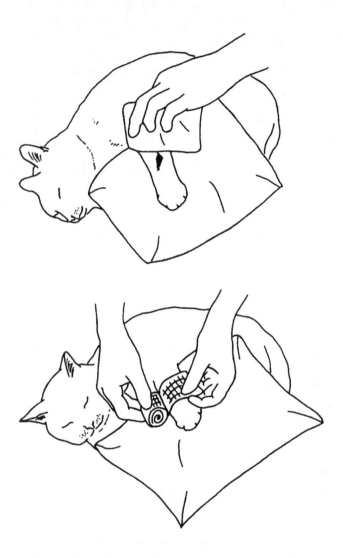

Figure 3-1: Top: To clean a bite wound, use a clean, soft cloth with soap and water. Wash from the center of the wound and move outward. Then rinse with water. Wear thick gloves if you suspect your cat was exposed to rabies. **Bottom:** Cover the bite wound with a pad that has antibiotic ointment on it, followed by gauze. Secure the gauze with adhesive tape (see Chapter 4, Section 2).

Both poisonous and nonpoisonous snakes are widely distributed over the United States. The poisonous snakes are the pit vipers (copperheads,

Agkistrodon contortrix; rattlesnakes, various species of *Crotalus* and *Sistrurus;* and cottonmouths, *Agkistrodon piscivorus*) and, to a lesser extent, the coral snakes (*Micruroides euryxanthus* and *Micrurus fulvius*). Table 3-1 lists the distribution of these snakes across the continental United States.

In general, bites from nonpoisonous snakes will look like scratches and won't cause much swelling, redness, or pain. The signs of a poisonous snakebite will largely depend on the location of the bite, how much venom is injected, and the general health and age of your cat. Most bites occur on the head and front legs. Sick, very young, and old cats may have a longer recovery time. Anaphylactic shock (see Chapter 3, Section 1) may occur in cats who are sensitive to the venom, but this is rare.

Table 3-1 Distribution of Poisonous Snakes in the Continental United States			
Copperheads	Alabama Arkansas Connecticut Delaware Florida Georgia Illinois Indiana Kansas	Kentucky Louisiana Maryland Massachusetts Mississippi Missouri New Jersey New York North Carolina	Ohio Oklahoma Pennsylvania South Carolina Tennessee Texas Virginia West Virginia
Coral Snakes	Alabama Arizona Arkansas Florida	Georgia Louisiana Mississippi New Mexico	North Carolina South Carolina Texas
Cottonmouths	Alabama Arkansas Florida Georgia Illinois	Kentucky Louisiana Mississippi Missouri North Carolina	Oklahoma South Carolina Tennessee Texas Virginia
Rattlesnakes	All states *except* Maine		

The signs of a poisonous snakebite are:

1. Swelling, pain, redness within 20 minutes at the site of the bite
2. Two fang marks (this may be difficult to see due to swelling)
3. Difficulty breathing, if bite is on the face or throat
4. Lameness, if the bite is on the leg
5. Vomiting
6. Diarrhea
7. Shallow breathing
8. Increased heart rate
9. Shock

FIRST AID

- *Keep your cat as still as possible—any movement will increase the absorption of the venom.* If possible, carry your cat instead of letting him walk.
- If you have access to a car, *immediately transport your cat to the nearest veterinary facility.* If you saw the snake, be able to describe it, as this will help in the choice of the antivenom. In particular, note the color of and pattern of any markings on the snake, and the presence or absence of a rattle. Do not approach or attempt to kill the snake.
- If your cat is having breathing difficulties, keep the airway open (see Figure 1-12).
- If a leg is bitten, keep it below the level of the heart (see Figure 3-2 [top left]) and apply pressure using your hand or a *flat* constricting band (*not a tourniquet*) between the bite and the heart (see Figure 3-2 [top right]). You can leave it on for as long as 2 hours. (Darkening of the skin below the band is an indication that the band is too tight.) Then, immobilize the leg with a splint (see Figure 3-2 [bottom] and Chapter 4, Section 3).
- Treat shock (see Chapter 1, Section 6).
- *Do not* wash the wound, as this may increase the absorption of the venom.
- *Do not* apply ice to the wound, as this may cause the skin to freeze and does not affect the spread of the venom.
- *Do not* make cuts over the wound and attempt to suck the venom out, as you may absorb some of the venom yourself.

NOTE: If you think the bite was from a nonpoisonous snake and you have access to a car, you should still transport your cat to a veterinary clinic immediately as he will have to be treated for any bacterial infections that may develop.

Figure 3-2: Top left: In the case of a snakebite on the leg, use a pillow placed under the cat's upper body to keep the affected leg below the level of the heart. **Top right:** For a snakebite on the leg, tie a piece of cloth or gauze around the leg between the bite and the cat's heart. The cloth should be snug but should allow one finger to fit under it. **Bottom:** To make a temporary splint, wrap a hand towel around the entire leg and then tape it closed.

Ticks

If your cat has ever been outside, especially in or near wooded areas, then he has been exposed to ticks. Ticks may be found anywhere on the cat but usually are attached to the head, neck, and between the toes. In this section, we will discuss Lyme disease, a tick disease that may affect cats.

Lyme Disease

Lyme disease has been reported in humans, horses, cattle, and dogs. This disease is rare in cats, and when they do become affected, it usually appears in a mild form.

This disease occurs when a tick of the genus *Ixodes* transmits a bacterium, *Borrelia burgorferi*, through its saliva while attached to a cat. The ticks that can transmit this disease are distributed in the Northeast (deer tick, *Ixodes dammini*), the West, the Midwest (California black-eyed tick, *Ixodes pacificus*), and the South (black-legged tick, *Ixodes scapularis*). The tick must be attached to the cat for at least one day before infection takes place. Once infection takes place, the following signs are seen:

1. Weakness
2. Sudden lameness
3. Loss of appetite
4. Fever
5. Depression
6. Reluctance to move

If you see any of the above signs, call your veterinarian. Although there is no first aid as such for Lyme disease, you may be able to prevent it by following several precautions:

- If you live in a wooded area, dust your cat lightly with flea/tick powder before letting him outdoors.
- When your cat returns, use your fingertips to comb through the fur over the entire body, starting at the head and moving back.
- If you find a tick, remove it with tweezers (Figure 2-3 [top]) or between your thumb and forefinger, pulling straight out (Figure 2-3 [bottom]). If possible, use a tissue or cloth when pulling to avoid exposure to the tick. Save it for your veterinarian to identify.

> **NOTE: A vaccine for the prevention of Lyme disease does exist, but it is recommended by the manufacturer for use in dogs only.**

Bees, Wasps, Hornets, and Ants

The stinging insects may pose a serious threat, especially if your cat is stung repeatedly or is hypersensitive to the venom (rare). The signs will vary with the location of the stings, the number of stings, and the sensitivity of your cat:

1. Pain and swelling in the area of the sting
2. Difficulty breathing, if the stings were in the mouth
3. Anaphylactic shock, if the cat is sensitized (see Section 1)
4. Shock, especially if there were multiple stings (see Chapter 1, Section 6)

FIRST AID

- *If shock develops, transport your cat to a veterinarian immediately after calling ahead. Treat for shock in the car.*
- Maintain an open airway if your cat has difficulty breathing (see Figure 1-12).
- If the leg is stung, make sure the leg remains below the level of the heart (see Figure 3-2 [top left]).
- Remove the embedded stinger with tweezers (see Figure 3-3 [left]) or by scraping with a credit card (see Figure 3-3 [right]). Do not squeeze the stinger because the venom sac may burst.
- Apply cold packs to the swollen area. *Do not use ice* because it may freeze the skin.
- Apply a paste of either baking soda and water or Adolf's instant meat tenderizer and water to the area of the sting to neutralize the venom.

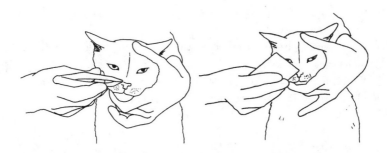

Figure 3-3: Left: To remove a stinger from the nose with tweezers, restrain your cat with one hand around the lower jaw, using the tweezers with your other hand. **Right:** To remove a stinger with a credit card, restrain your cat with one hand around the lower jaw. Carefully scrape the surface of the nose with a credit card by rubbing it back and forth until the stinger is removed.

Spiders

Only two types of spiders are capable of causing severe injury to your cat: the female black widow (*Lactrodectus mactans*) and the brown recluse (*Loxoscles reclusus*).

The black widow is a shiny black spider, about three quarters of an inch in length, with a red hourglass-shaped spot on its underside. The brown recluse is a tawny to brown spider, about half an inch in length, with long legs and a dark brown fiddle-shaped mark on its back. The black widow is found all over the United States, and the brown recluse is found mainly in the southern United States.

Black Widow
The signs of a black widow bite are:

1. Severe pain at the site of the bite
2. Muscle spasms
3. Drooling
4. Convulsions
5. Difficulty breathing
6. Paralysis (may happen early and be severe)

· FIRST AID

- Keep your cat still until seen by a veterinarian and treated with antivenom, if available.
- If the leg has been bitten, keep the leg below the level of the heart (see Figure 3-2 [top left]).
- Watch for signs of allergic reactions (see Chapter 3, Section 1).
- Maintain an open airway (see Figure 1-12).

Brown Recluse
The signs associated with a brown recluse bite are:

1. Initially, little pain or swelling associated with the bite will be present.
2. After a few hours, a blister will form.
3. After one to two weeks, an ulcer will develop.

4. Fever
5. Joint pain
6. Anemia

No specific first aid is necessary; however, once you recognize the signs, it is important that the blister or ulcer be surgically removed as soon as possible so that the surrounding skin is not affected. Recovery may take weeks to months.

Scorpions

Two dangerous species of scorpions are found in the United States (sculptured centroides—*Centruroides sculpturatus*—and *Vejovis spinigerus*), and both live in southern Arizona. The stinger, which contains the venom, is on the last segment of the tail. The signs associated with scorpion stings are:

1. Extreme pain, swelling, and redness at the site of the sting
2. Drooling
3. Generalized weakness
4. Paralysis
5. Breathing difficulties

FIRST AID

- Bring your cat to your veterinarian immediately for supportive treatment and an injection of antivenom.
- Apply cold packs on the sting, if possible. Do not use ice because it may freeze the skin.
- If your cat has breathing difficulties, maintain an open airway until your cat can be seen by your veterinarian (see Chapter 1, Figure 1-12).

Lizards

Fortunately for cats, lizards are not very aggressive and the biting incidence is low. Only two species of poisonous lizards are found in the United States: the Gila monster (*Heloderma suspectum*) and the Mexican beaded lizard

(*Heloderma horidunium*). Both species have a yellow or coral-colored pattern to their beadlike skin and both are found in the southwestern United States. The signs associated with lizard bites are:

1. Intense pain and swelling at the site of the bite
2. Drooling
3. Vomiting
4. Shock

FIRST AID

- Remove the lizard, by prying open the jaws with pliers, if it does not let go.
- Flush the wound with plenty of water.
- Treat for shock (see Chapter 1, Section 6) on the way to your veterinarian.

SECTION 5: BURNS

Most cases of burns in cats are due to heat injury from a heating pad, a heat lamp, or hot liquid accidentally spilled on them. Also, cats who jump up on kitchen stoves and wood-burning stoves may suffer burns to their feet and tails. Kittens and playful cats who chew on electric cords may experience a burned mouth or worse, electric shock (see Section 8). Chemical injury (from acid and alkali cleaners) may also cause burns to the skin or mouth. If your cat becomes trapped in a burning building, smoke inhalation may cause burns to the lining of the breathing passages and the eyes.

When severe, burns may cause shock, extreme pain, and infection. The severity depends on the age of the cat and the size, location, and depth of the burn. Burns are considered serious when they affect very young or very old cats, when they are spread over more than about 15 percent of the cat's body, when they occur on the head or joints, or when the full thickness of the skin is destroyed. The signs of a burn injury on the skin will mostly depend upon the depth of the burn. These are classified as:

Superficial or First Degree

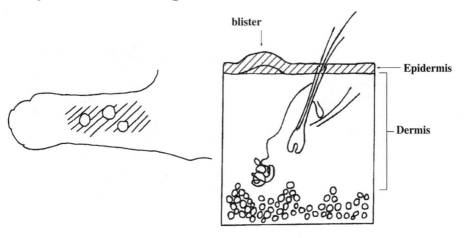

Figure 3-4: In a superficial or first-degree burn, the injury to the skin is confined to the epidermis, which appears red and may blister. It will heal rapidly in most cases.

Partial Thickness or Second Degree

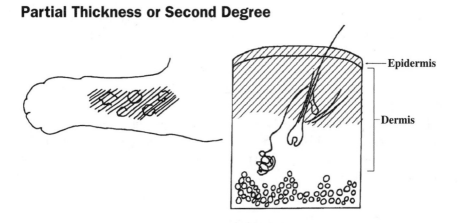

Figure 3-5: In a partial or second-degree burn, the injury to the skin involves the epidermis and part of the dermis. Any blisters are broken and the surface initially appears red, wet, and swollen. In a few days, it will dry to a tan-colored crust. This burn typically heals in about two weeks if treated.

Full Thickness or Third Degree

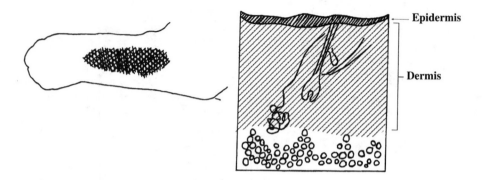

Figure 3-6: In a full or third-degree burn, the injury extends to both layers of the skin and may extend under the skin. The surface appears blackened, and there is no hair. It will heal very slowly with a scar unless a skin graft is done.

In general you should *never put ice, oils, or ointments on the burn,* because ice can freeze the tissue and ointments are difficult to remove. Also, *ointments or sprays containing the ingredient benzocaine are toxic to a cat* and should never be used under any circumstances (see Section 9). You should also never use cotton or any material that has loose fibers to cover the burn, because fibers sticking to the burned tissue may be difficult to remove.

First-aid methods will vary according to the type of burn; but for all burns other than a superficial heat burn, you should see your veterinarian immediately. If you are not sure of the type of burn your cat has suffered, have it assessed by your veterinarian.

FIRST AID: HEAT BURNS

Superficial
- Clean gently with soap and water (see Figure 3-1 [top]).
- Apply cool compresses for 30 minutes (see Figure 3-7).
- Cover with a bandage (see Figure 3-1 [bottom] and Chapter 4, Section 2).

Partial or Full Thickness
- Treat shock.
- Cover with a loose bandage (see Figure 3-1 [bottom] and Chapter 4, Section 2).

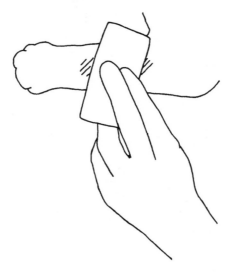

Figure 3-7: Apply a cool compress to the superficial burn.

FIRST AID: CHEMICAL BURNS

- Remove contaminated collars or harnesses.
- Flush with cool running water for at least 20 minutes (see Figure 3-8 [top] and Figure 2-6).
- Cover with a bandage (see Figure 3-8 [bottom], and Chapter 4, Section 2).

FIRST AID: SMOKE INHALATION BURNS

- Remove your cat from the source of smoke.
- Observe carefully for difficulty breathing, especially within the first 24 hours after the incident.

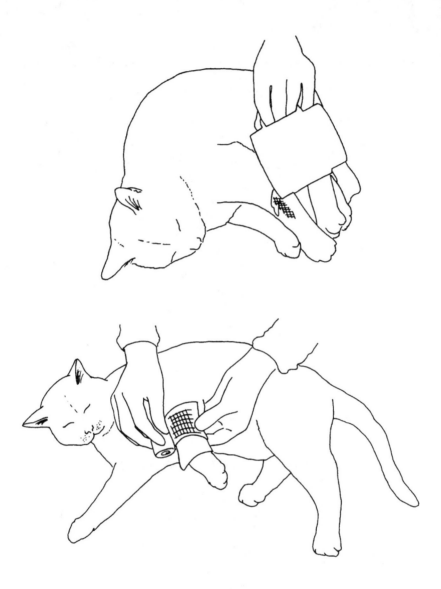

Figure 3-8: Top: To flush a chemical burn, pour cool water from a cup or use a hose turned on low volume. **Bottom:** To cover a chemical burn, place a pad on the burn and cover loosely, first with gauze and then with adhesive (see Chapter 4, Section 2).

SECTION 6: COMA

Coma occurs when your cat has a complete loss of consciousness, as in sleep, but has no response to pain. It can be caused by an underlying disease in many different organs: brain, heart, kidney, liver, lung, and pancreas. It may also be caused by certain drugs, poisons, temperature extremes, shock, and infections. Because there are so many causes, some of which may cause death in a very short period of time, it is very important to recognize the signs and *provide first aid while on the way to your veterinarian.* The two major signs of coma are:

1. Sleeplike appearance
2. No response to pain

FIRST AID

- Keep an airway open at all times.
- Monitor and provide CPR, if necessary, until your cat can be examined

SECTION 7: DIABETIC EMERGENCIES

These emergencies can occur when either too much insulin (causing low blood sugar) or too little insulin (causing high blood sugar) is given when treating a diabetic cat. In both cases, your veterinarian should be notified immediately.

Too Much Insulin

The signs begin about 3 to 7 hours after the last dose of insulin and include:

1. Weakness
2. Fatigue
3. Seizures
4. Coma

- Keep a bottle of a glucose-containing syrup (for example, Karo® syrup) available and get an appropriate dosage from your veterinarian in case you need to use it.
- If convulsions start, *do not* attempt to pour the syrup into the cat's mouth, as the animal will choke. Instead, give the syrup as shown in Figure 3-9. Be careful not to get bitten.

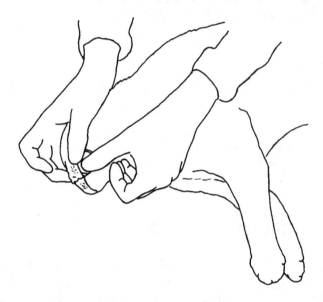

Figure 3-9: To rub a glucose-containing syrup on your cat's gums, place one hand over your cat's muzzle and lift the lip with your thumb. Pour some syrup on the thumb of your other hand and rub this into the gums.

Too Little Insulin

If you have forgotten to give your cat an insulin injection or have given too little, you may notice the following signs:

1. Depression
2. Increased drinking and urination

3. Weakness
4. Sweet, fruity smell to the breath
5. Vomiting
6. Coma

FIRST AID

- Give your cat the normal dose of insulin immediately.

    NOTE: If your cat is not being treated for diabetes and is showing the signs described above, he may have diabetes. Have the animal examined by your veterinarian.

SECTION 8: ELECTRIC SHOCK

In most cases, electric shock is caused by chewing on an electric cord. A typical household AC outlet has a frequency of 60 Hz. When your cat contacts an exposed wire, his heart will beat erratically and his lungs will fill with fluid. The signs will be:

1. Difficulty breathing
2. Burns in and around the mouth
3. Loss of consciousness
4. Heart stops

FIRST AID

- If your cat still has the electric cord in his mouth, pull the plug out before providing first aid.
- Provide CPR support as needed on the way to the veterinarian.
- Treat burns around the mouth if possible with cool compresses (not ice; see Figure 3-10).
- Monitor respiration and pulse rates often, especially during the first 12 hours following the accident.

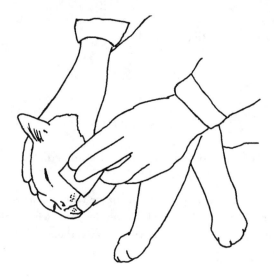

Figure 3-10: To treat burns around the mouth, hold a cool compress on the injured area.

SECTION 9: POISONING

Cats may be poisoned by many substances in our environment. The causes range from common household items such as insecticides, cleaning solutions, and antifreeze to the seeds, bark, and leaves of many different plants. Cats may even be poisoned by mouthing or biting certain toads and salamanders. It is important to remember that all human drugs, even common household medicines such as aspirin and acetaminophen (Tylenol®), may poison your cat. *Always check with your veterinarian* before *giving or using any medicine on your cat.* The signs from any type of poison will mostly depend on the quantity ingested, but in general you should suspect that your cat has been poisoned if you see the following signs occur *suddenly:*

1. Excess salivation
2. Vomiting
3. Fatigue
4. Convulsions

If you believe that your cat has been poisoned, call your veterinarian or the National Animal Poison Control Center immediately (see General First Aid, below). Table 3-2 lists the common poisons, their major sources, and the first aid required when these poisons are ingested or inhaled. For cases of external poisoning (for example, a spill on the fur or an overdose of flea powder) involving the chemicals listed in Table 3-2, see General First Aid below. Table 3-3 details plant poisoning by common name/toxic part, the signs, and first aid. Poisonings from toads and salamanders are discussed following the General First Aid section.

Table 3-2
Common Poisons

Poison	Source	First Aid for Ingested or Inhaled Poisons
Acids	cleaning solutions etching solutions household chlorine bleach	1. DO NOT INDUCE VOMITING. 2. Rinse out mouth with water. 3. Give 1 to 2 tablespoons of cooking oil or mineral oil, once.
Alkalis	ammonia washing powders paint removers laundry detergents	1. DO NOT INDUCE VOMITING. 2. Rinse out mouth with water. 3. Give 1 to 2 tablespoons of cooking oil, or mineral oil, once.
Arsenic	insecticides herbicides paint	1. Induce vomiting. 2. Give activated charcoal. *Antidote available from veterinarian*
Carbamates	insecticides: Carbaryl® Sevin® Propoxur®	1. Induce vomiting. 2. Give activated charcoal. *Antidote available from veterinarian*
Carbon monoxide	exhaust fumes	1. Remove the cat from the source of fumes. 2. Give CPR, if necessary. 3. Monitor closely for 48 hours.
Chocolate	milk chocolate baking chocolate cocoa powder	1. Induce vomiting. 2. Give activated charcoal.

Poison	Source	First Aid for Ingested or Inhaled Poisons
Drugs (human)	aspirin acetaminophen (Tylenol®) benzocaine ibuprofen (Advil®)	1. Induce vomiting. 2. Give activated charcoal. *Antidote available* *from veterinarian* *for acetaminophen*
Ethylene glycol	antifreeze film-processing solutions solvents rust removers	1. Induce vomiting. 2. Give activated charcoal. *Antidote available* *from veterinarian*
Lead	ceramics batteries fishing sinkers golf balls insecticides linoleum paint	1. Induce vomiting. 2. Give activated charcoal. *Antidote available* *from veterinarian*
Metaldehyde	rodenticide snail bait	1. Induce vomiting. 2. Give activated charcoal.

Organophosphates	insecticides:
	  Dichlorvos®
	  Fenthion®
	  Parathion®
	  Ronnel®
	  Trichlorfon®
		1. Induce vomiting.
		2. Give activated charcoal.
		Antidote available
		from veterinarian

Petroleum distillates	motor oil gasoline turpentine paint paint thinner paint remover lighter fluid kerosene	1. DO NOT INDUCE VOMITING. 2. Give 1 to 2 tablespoons of cooking oil or mineral oil, once.
Phenol	disinfectants (Lysol®) fungicides herbicides wood preservatives photographic developers	*If there are no signs of burns in the mouth:* 1. Induce vomiting. 2. Give activated charcoal. *If there are burns in the mouth:* 1. DO NOT INDUCE VOMITING. 2. Rinse the mouth with water. 3. Give 1 to 2 tablespoons of cooking oil or mineral oil, once.

Poison	Source	First Aid for Ingested or Inhaled Poisons
Strychnine	rodenticides	1. Induce vomiting only if there are no signs of breathing difficulty or seizures. 2. Give activated charcoal.
Vitamin D₃ (Cholecalciferol)	rodenticides	1. Induce vomiting. 2. Give activated charcoal. 3. Keep cat out of sunlight. *Antidote available from veterinarian*
Warfarin	rodenticide	1. Induce vomiting. 2. Give activated charcoal. *Antidote available from veterinarian*
Zinc	pennies made since 1983 paint nails/metal objects zinc oxide skin preps Calamine® lotion Desenex®	1. Induce vomiting. 2. Give activated charcoal.

Table 3-3
Poisonous Plants

Common Name/ Toxic Part	Symptoms	First Aid
almond/seeds	cyanide poisoning: bright red gums, involuntary urination and defecation, labored breathing, convulsions, frothing at the mouth, coma	1. Induce vomiting. 2. Give activated charcoal. *Antidote available from veterinarian*
amaryllis/bulb	depression, vomiting	1. Induce vomiting. 2. Give activated charcoal.
apple/seeds	cyanide poisoning: bright red gums, involuntary urination and defecation, labored breathing, convulsions, frothing at the mouth, coma	1. Induce vomiting. 2. Give activated charcoal. *Antidote available from veterinarian*
apricot/seeds	cyanide poisoning: bright red gums, involuntary urination and defecation, labored breathing, convulsions, frothing at the mouth, coma	1. Induce vomiting. 2. Give activated charcoal. *Antidote available from veterinarian*
azalea/leaf	repeated swallowing, excess saliva	1. Induce vomiting. 2. Give activated charcoal.

Common Name/ Toxic Part	Symptoms	First Aid
bitter cherry/ seeds	cyanide poisoning: bright red gums, involuntary urination and defecation, labored breathing, convulsions, frothing at the mouth, coma	1. Induce vomiting. 2. Give activated chacoal. *Antidote available* *from veterinarian*
blackberry/hooked barbs of stems	punctures and lacerations of eye, mouth, skin, and feet	1. Clean and treat wounds. 2. Bandage.
black night-shade/berries	vomiting, bloody diarrhea, trembling, weakness	1. Induce vomiting. 2. Give activated charcoal.
black walnuts/ hulls	vomiting, diarrhea, convulsions	1. Induce vomiting 2. Give activated charcoal.
bull nettles/ hair all over plant	burning in mouth, muscle weakness, slow and irregular heartbeat	1. Keep cat quiet. 2. DO NOT INDUCE VOMITING.
burdock/hooked barbs of florets	lacerate eyes, ears, nose, trachea, bronchus	1. Clean and treat wounds. 2. Bandage. 3. Keep airway open. 4. CPR if necessary.
cactus/sharp spines of leaf	multiple punctures with migrating spine fragments	1. Clean and treat wounds. 2. Bandage. 3. Remove by clipping all spines that are caught in the hair. 4. All migrating parts must be removed surgically.
castor bean/bean	fever, profuse bloody diarrhea	1. Induce vomiting. 2. Give activated charcoal. 3. Monitor for signs of shock.
choke cherry/ seeds	cyanide poisoning: bright red gums, involuntary urination and defecation, labored breathing, convulsions, frothing at the mouth, coma	1. Induce vomiting. 2. Give activated charcoal. *Antidote available* *from veterinarian*
climbing night-shade/berries	vomiting, bloody diarrhea, trembling, weakness	1. Induce vomiting. 2. Give activated charcoal.
crown-of-thorns/ irritant sap in leaves	inflammation to skin and eye, vomiting, diarrhea	1. Induce vomiting. 2. Give activated charcoal.
daffodil/bulb	depression, vomiting	1. Induce vomiting. 2. Give activated charcoal.
dewberry/hooked barbs of stems	punctures and lacerations of eye, mouth, skin, and feet	1. Clean and treat wounds. 2. Bandage.
dumb cane/ leaves	swelling of the tongue and throat, difficulty breathing	1. Keep airway open. 2. CPR if necessary. 3. DO NOT INDUCE VOMITING.

Common Name/ Toxic Part	Symptoms	First Aid
Easter lily/flow- ers, stems, leaves	excessive drinking and urination, kidney failure	1. Induce vomiting. 2. Give activated charcoal.
elephant ears/ leaves	swelling of the tongue and throat, difficulty breathing	1. Keep airway open. 2. CPR if necessary. 3. DO NOT INDUCE VOMITING.
English ivy/fruit	intense thirst, vomiting, diarrhea, may die within 1 to 2 days	1. Induce vomiting. 2. Give activated charcoal.
English walnuts/ hulls	vomiting, diarrhea, convulsions	1. Induce vomiting. 2. Give activated charcoal.
purple fox- glove/all parts	depression, bloody diarrhea, fast or slow heartbeat	1. Induce vomiting. 2. Give activated charcoal.

**grasses (foxtail,
wild barley, june
grass, ripgut
grass)/awns, barbs,
fragmented seed
heads**
	barbs penetrate and migrate into
	ear canal, air passages, under
	skin, and into body cavities
		1. Clean and treat wounds.
		2. Bandage.
		3. Remove by clipping all
		   spines, awns, barbs, or
		   seed heads that are
		   caught in the hair.
		4. All migrating parts
		   must be removed surgically.

hawthorn/heavy spines on stems	stab wounds of eye, skin, feet, legs	1. Clean and treat wounds. 2. Bandage.
honey locust/ pronged spines	eye lacerations and puncture wounds of skin	1. Clean and treat wounds. 2. Bandage
iris/bulb	depression, vomiting	1. Induce vomiting. 2. Give activated charcoal.
japanese yew/ needles, bark, seed	muscular weakness, difficulty breathing	1. Induce vomiting. 2. Give activated charcoal. 3. Keep airway open. 4. Give CPR if necessary.
Jerusalem cherry/ berries	vomiting, bloody diarrhea, trembling, weakness	1. Induce vomiting. 2. Give activated charcoal.
jimsonweed/seeds	dry, red skin; fever; convulsions	1. Induce vomiting. 2. Give activated charcoal.
lily-of-the-valley/ bulb	depression, bloody diarrhea, fast or slow heartbeat	1. Induce vomiting. 2. Give activated charcoal.
mistletoe/berries	vomiting, diarrhea	1. Induce vomiting. 2. Give activated charcoal.
mushroom poisoning (family: Amanifaceae)/cap	vomiting, diarrhea, muscle spasms	1. Induce vomiting. 2. Give activated charcoal.
nettle spurge/ hair all over plant	burning in mouth, muscle weakness, slow and irregular heartbeat	1. Keep cat quiet. 2. DO NOT INDUCE VOMITING.

85

Common Name/ Toxic Part	Symptoms	First Aid
oleander (very toxic)/ leaf, bark, stems	depression, bloody diarrhea, fast or slow heartbeat	1. Induce vomiting. 2. Give activated charcoal.
onion/bulbs, flowers, stems	vomiting, diarrhea, weakness, anemia, liver damage	1. Induce vomiting. 2. Give activated charcoal.
osage orange/heavy spines on stems	stab wounds of eye, skin, feet, legs	1. Clean and treat wounds. 2. Bandage.
philodendron/leaves	swelling of the tongue and throat, difficulty breathing	1. Keep airway open. 2. CPR if necessary. 3. DO NOT INDUCE VOMITING.
poinsettia/irritant sap in leaves	inflammation to skin and eye, vomiting, diarrhea	1. Induce vomiting. 2. Give activated charcoal.
precatory bean/bean	fever, profuse bloody diarrhea	1. Induce vomiting. 2. Give activated charcoal. 3. Monitor for signs of shock.
quince/heavy spines on stems	stab wounds of eye, skin, feet, legs	1. Clean and treat wounds. 2. Bandage.
rhododendrons/ leaf	repeated swallowing, excess saliva	1. Induce vomiting. 2. Give activated charcoal.
rose/hooked barbs of stems	punctures and lacerations of eye, mouth, skin, and feet	1. Clean and treat wounds. 2. Bandage.
skunk cabbage/leaves	swelling of the tongue and throat, difficulty breathing	1. Keep airway open. 2. CPR if necessary. 3. DO NOT INDUCE VOMITING.
snow-on-the-mountain/ irritant sap in the leaves	inflammation to skin and eye, vomiting, diarrhea	1. Induce vomiting. 2. Give activated charcoal.
stinging nettle/ hair all over plant	burning in mouth, muscle weakness, slow and irregular heartbeat	1. Keep cat quiet. 2. DO NOT INDUCE VOMITING.
tinsel tree-milk bush/ irritant sap in the leaves	inflammation to skin and eye, vomiting, diarrhea	1. Induce vomiting. 2. Give activated charcoal.
tobacco/leaves	vomiting, diarrhea, difficulty breathing, staggering, weakness	1. Induce vomiting. 2. Give activated charcoal. 3. Keep airway open. 4. Give CPR if necessary.
tulip/bulb	depression, vomiting	1. Induce vomiting. 2. Give activated charcoal.
wild black cherry/ seeds	cyanide poisoning: bright red gums, involuntary urination and defecation, labored breathing, convulsions, frothing at the mouth, coma	1. Induce vomiting. 2. Give activated charcoal. *Antidote available from veterinarian*

General First Aid for Poisoning

1. If your cat is unconscious, check the airway, breathing, and circulation, and perform CPR as necessary.
2. Call your veterinarian and be ready to tell her or him what the poison is, what the active ingredients are (if you know them), how much was eaten, when it was eaten, and what signs your cat is showing.
3. If your veterinarian cannot be reached, call the National Animal Poison Control Center at one of the following numbers:

   - 1-900-680-0000
   - 1-800-548-2423

These numbers are answered 24 hours a day, 7 days a week. There is a charge for these services.

4. Take the following steps for poison ingested within the past 2 hours:

   - If your cat is conscious and you know the poison is *not* a petroleum product, cleaning solution, or a strong acid or alkali, induce vomiting using either 3 percent hydrogen peroxide (at a dosage of 1 teaspoon by mouth; if no vomiting occurs within 15 minutes, repeat only once) or syrup of ipecac (at a dosage of 1 to 2 teaspoons by mouth given once). See Appendix 2, Figure A-1 [top] for how to administer these agents.
   - Inspect the vomit and save a sample for your veterinarian.
   - Once vomiting has occurred, activated charcoal (at a dosage of 0.5 grams of activated charcoal per pound of body weight) may be given to absorb the remaining toxin. Activated charcoal is much more effective if given in a liquid form. To make a liquid paste from the powder form, mix 1 gram of charcoal to 1 to 2 teaspoons of water and administer via a medicine dropper (see Appendix 2, Figure A-1 [top]).
   - If you are unable to induce vomiting in your cat and are unable to have your cat seen by a veterinarian soon, give activated charcoal as described above.

5. With the exception of paint, tar, motor oil, and similar substances, most poisons that are not taken internally and therefore

remain on the outside of your cat can be removed by following these steps:

- Flush the area with large amounts of water for at least 5 minutes.
- Wear gloves and wash your cat with mild soap and water.
- Dry well to prevent chilling.

6. To remove paint, tar, or motor oil from the fur or skin of your cat:

- Wearing gloves, rub in large amounts of mineral oil or vegetable oil before the poisons harden.
- After the poisons become loosened, bathe your cat in warm water made soapy with a mild dishwashing liquid, like Dawn®.
- Rinse well, repeat if necessary.
- In severe cases, dust your cat with cornmeal, cornstarch, or flour after you have rubbed in the mineral oil. This will help to remove more of the toxin. To remove, comb or brush your cat and bathe in warm, soapy water.
- *Remember* not *to use turpentine, paint thinner, or mineral spirits to remove the paint, tar, or motor oil.* These substances are very toxic to your cat.

Toads and Salamanders

As mentioned above, cats may become poisoned by biting or mouthing certain toads and salamanders. Kittens are the most susceptible to severe reactions.

Toads
Two species of toads in the United States can poison cats: Colorado River toads (*Bufo alvarius*) and marine toads (*Bufo marinus*). The Colorado River toads are found in the Southwest, and the marine toads are found in Florida.
The signs seen in toad poisoning occur rapidly and are:

1. Profuse salivation
2. Difficulty breathing
3. Heart rhythm abnormalities
4. Convulsions
5. Prostration

FIRST AID

- Flush mouth with large quantities of water (see Figure 2-6).
- Maintain an open airway (see Figure 1-12).
- Give CPR, if necessary (see Chapter 1, Section 3).

Salamanders

The California newt (*Taricha torosa*) is the only species of poisonous salamander in the United States. It is found in California.

The signs that your cat has been in contact with one are:

1. Weakness and incoordination
2. Paralysis

FIRST AID

- Cats usually recover quickly without treatment.
- You can help your cat recover more quickly by washing his mouth with large quantities of water (see Figure 2-6).

SECTION 10: SEIZURES

Seizures occur when there is a sudden disturbance in brain function. If this disturbance spreads to a specific area of the brain, the seizure is said to be partial; if it spreads to a broad area of the brain, the seizure is said to be generalized. Seizures have many causes, including sudden trauma, lack of thiamine (vitamin B_1) in the diet, high body temperature, brain tumor, lack of oxygen, low blood sugar, liver disease, viruses, or poisons. Sometimes, however, they have no known cause and are called idiopathic. If the seizures recur, the condition is known as epilepsy.

Partial Seizures

The signs seen will depend on the type of seizure. If the seizure is partial, you might see either:

1. Convulsions limited to a specific area of the body (for example, the right front leg)

2. Specific behavioral changes such as sudden blindness, running wildly, howling, self-mutilation (e.g., tail biting), or eating non-food items

Generalized Seizures

The most common generalized seizure is the *grand mal,* which consists of four stages:

1. Aura: This is the time just before the seizure. Your cat will be restless and anxious and may want to be close to you. This will last 1 to 2 minutes.
2. Prodome: This is the stage at which your cat loses consciousness; it will last for 1 to 2 seconds.
3. Ictus: In this stage, your cat will remain unconscious and will have convulsions accompanied by vocalization, urination, defecation, drooling, and dilated pupils. This stage lasts from a few seconds to a few minutes.
4. Postictal: At this stage, your cat will regain consciousness and may show blindness, confusion, and weakness. It can last from a few hours to a few days.

FIRST AID

- As soon as you notice the aura stage, immediately engage your cat in an activity he likes. This may prevent a seizure.
- If convulsions start, make sure the ground is smooth and clear of all objects that the cat may hit during the seizure.
- Do not attempt to hold your cat's mouth open or shut.
- After the convulsions, keep the cat confined and monitor the breathing and pulse (see Chapter 1, Section 1). Schedule an appointment with your veterinarian for a complete exam of your cat.
- Keep a good record of all seizures your cat has had. Note the time of day and date, the number of hours after a meal, and anything unusual that coincided with the event. This will help your veterinarian in trying to find a cause and in recommending treatment.
- You should notify your veterinarian *immediately* if:

(a) The seizures occur one after another, with little or no period of rest in between. This condition is called status epilepticus and is a major emergency.

(b) The seizure lasts for more than a few minutes.

SECTION 11: TEMPERATURE EXTREMES

Cats exposed to very high or very low environmental temperatures may suffer drastic changes in their own body temperatures. How much the body temperature changes will greatly depend on the extent and duration of exposure as well as the age and physical condition of the cat. In general, very young and very old cats are most sensitive to temperature extremes. It is important to note that both temperature extremes can cause seizures, coma, and death.

Heat stroke, eclampsia, and seizure disorders can all cause your cat's body temperature to be very high (above 105°F).

Heat Stroke—High Temperatures

Heat stroke most often occurs when cats are confined in unventilated buildings or cars during hot weather. Some of the initial signs are:

1. Panting
2. Increased pulse
3. Bright red gums
4. High body temperature (105° to 110°F)

Later signs will be:

1. Stupor
2. Shock
3. Pale gums
4. Vomiting
5. Diarrhea

Final signs are:

1. Coma
2. No breathing

FIRST AID

- Move your cat to a cool, ventilated area.
- If necessary, give CPR and treat for shock on the way to your veterinarian.
- Give your cat a cold- or ice-water bath.
- Take a rectal temperature every 10 minutes.
- Stop the bath when the temperature reaches 103°F.
- *Do not give aspirin or acetaminophen.*

Eclampsia and Seizures—High Temperatures

In these conditions, body temperatures become very high due to heat produced through muscle movement. Eclampsia refers to the muscle tremors that may occur in the female cat after giving birth. In seizures, especially those which are clustered together or prolonged, the muscle action during the convulsions can cause high body temperatures (see Seizures, Section 10).

FIRST AID

- Take the temperature. In a case of eclampsia, first remove the kittens from the mother. In a case of seizures, wait until your cat has stopped having convulsions before taking the temperature.
- If the temperature is above 105°F, start cold- or ice-water baths as for heat stroke.
- Take a rectal temperature every 10 minutes.
- Stop the bath when the temperature reaches 103°F.
- Have your cat examined by your veterinarian to be sure he does not need further treatment.

Exposure to extremely cold weather can produce generalized body chilling to temperatures of 77° to 95°F (and sometimes lower). This condition is called hypothermia. Cold exposure may also produce frostbite, which is a freezing of small areas of the body. Sometimes, both hypothermia and frostbite occur together.

Hypothermia—Low Temperatures

The major signs seen in hypothermia are:

1. Low body temperatures (below 95°F)
2. Very slow pulse rate
3. Very slow breathing rate
4. Seizures
5. Coma

FIRST AID

- Give a warm water bath or wrap your cat in blankets in a warm room. Use blankets that have been warmed in a dryer for a few minutes.
- Take a rectal temperature every 10 minutes.
- Stop the bath when the temperature reaches 101°F.
- *Beware of hot water bottles, heat lamps, and electric blankets, as these may burn the skin.*

Frostbite—Low Temperatures

Mild cases of frostbite have the following signs:

1. Skin will first appear pale.
2. Skin later becomes red, hot, painful, and swollen.
3. Skin will eventually return to normal but will always be extra sensitive.

Severe cases of frostbite have the following signs:

1. Skin stays cold and starts to shrivel.
2. Skin will eventually slough, leaving behind a raw wound.

FIRST AID

Mild frostbite
- Warm the frostbitten area rapidly with a water bath between 105°F and 108°F for about 15 minutes.

- Cover with a loose bandage (see Chapter 4, Section 2).
- Do not rub the skin.

Severe frostbite
- Treat as mild frostbite.
- Tissue that is devitalized must be removed by your veterinarian.

SECTION 12: THROMBOEMBOLISM

Thromboembolism occurs when a clot, forming in a heart chamber or blood vessel, becomes lodged in a vessel as it circulates through the body. The occurrence of thromboembolism is very often associated with heart disease. The circulating clot may become lodged anywhere but oftentimes becomes stuck in the distal aorta, which is the large blood vessel that supplies the lower half of the body. The signs of this sort of thromboembolism are:

1. Weakness in the hind limbs
2. Painful, cold, pale hind limbs
3. No femoral pulses (see Chapter 1, Section 1)
4. Yowling while lying on side

While there is no first aid as such for thromboembolism, it is very important to recognize the signs and *have your cat seen immediately by a veterinarian.*

SECTION 13: URINARY TRACT BLOCKAGE

Blockage of the urinary tract occurs mostly in male cats. The urethra, which connects the bladder with the external opening in the penis, is quite narrow and long and may consequently become blocked. Most often, blockage is caused by uroliths, which are small stones composed of mineral salts, or urethral plugs, which contain a matrix material in addition to mineral salts. As the urethral plugs or uroliths pass through the urinary tract, they may become caught in the urethra and prevent urine from leaving the bladder. Blockage or the signs of blockage may also be caused by the presence of tumors, infection, inflammation, or nerve malfunction in the urinary tract. The major signs are:

1. Frequent attempts to urinate
2. Straining to urinate
3. Bloody urine
4. Dehydration
5. Shock

FIRST AID

- If you see the signs described above, have your cat examined immediately.
- Treat for shock (see Chapter 1, Section 6).

SECTION 14: VESTIBULAR SYNDROME

Feline vestibular syndrome is a disorder that occurs suddenly and affects your cat's state of balance. It usually occurs in summer and early fall and has no known cause. Cats that experience this syndrome are healthy in all respects but will show the following signs:

1. Head tilted to one side
2. Disorientation
3. Rolling
4. Falling
5. Involuntary rapid movement of the eyeballs

A severely affected cat may be so disoriented that movement is impossible. In place of a head tilt, a cat may swing his head in wide excursions. This may be accompanied by vocalizing.

There is no first aid treatment for this condition. To be sure there are no underlying causes of disease (for example, ear infection, tumors in the ear, trauma to the ear), you should have your cat examined by your veterinarian. Cats affected by this syndrome usually spontaneously improve in 72 hours and are back to normal in 2 to 3 weeks, although a head tilt may persist for some time.

SECTION 15: VOMITING AND DIARRHEA

Vomiting and diarrhea are considered together because they share many of the same causes and signs; the first aid for the two conditions is nearly identical.

Vomiting

A change in diet (new food or eating garbage), intestinal parasites, contagious viral diseases, and foreign objects in the stomach or intestine are some of the major causes of vomiting in cats of all ages. Cats who groom themselves excessively will have occasional bouts of vomiting from hairballs. In kittens, sudden vomiting may also be caused by an intussusception, which occurs when one part of the intestine pushes into the inside of another part. In more mature cats, any of the following may also cause vomiting: liver disease, kidney disease, diabetes, ulcers, poisons, inflammatory bowel disease, and gastrointestinal tumors. The signs that your cat may be about to vomit are:

1. Drooling
2. Excessive swallowing
3. Abdominal contractions (retching)
4. Pacing and restlessness

Vomiting may then cause:

1. Weakness
2. Dehydration
3. Shock (if vomiting is severe)

Diarrhea

Diarrhea occurs when the frequency and the fluid content of the bowel movement are increased. The major causes of diarrhea are abrupt diet changes, intestinal parasites, contagious viral diseases, inflammatory bowel disease, drugs (antibiotics and anticancer drugs), stress, and poisons. A hyperactive thyroid gland may also cause diarrhea in the cat. The signs seen with diarrhea are the same as vomiting:

1. Weakness
2. Dehydration
3. Shock (if diarrhea is severe)

FIRST AID

- *First check to see if your cat is dehydrated* (see Figures 1-4 and 1-5).
- If your cat is dehydrated, notify your veterinarian at once, as this condition could easily lead to shock.
- If your cat is not dehydrated and is vomiting, confine the animal and withhold food and water for 12 to 24 hours. You can offer ice cubes for your cat to lick (see note below).
- If your cat is not dehydrated and has diarrhea but is not vomiting, confine him and withhold food for 12 to 24 hours. You can offer small amounts of water during this time.
- Note what the vomit/diarrhea looks like and save some in an airtight container in your refrigerator for your veterinarian to examine.
- If your cat has had no vomiting/diarrhea after 12 to 24 hours, you can offer 1 to 2 tablespoons of broth or baby food every 3 hours. If your cat continues without vomiting/diarrhea, increase these foods and gradually introduce the standard fare over the next two to three days.
- Notify your veterinarian in any of the following situations: if vomiting/diarrhea persists during the 12 to 24 hours when food and water are restricted, if vomiting/diarrhea begins again with eating and drinking, if you find blood in the vomit/diarrhea, or if shock develops (see Chapter 1, Section 6).
- Treat for shock if necessary (see Chapter 1, Section 6).

> **NOTE: Never withhold water from a cat with impaired kidney function; instead, see your veterinarian immediately. Also, if your cat is vomiting hairballs only, you should not withhold food or water. Call your veterinarian to discuss this problem.**

SUMMARY

The emergencies listed in this chapter require action within a few minutes to a few hours if your cat is not to suffer severe illness or loss of life. An important first step is being able to recognize the signs of each emergency. Often, if the emergency is recognized sufficiently early and the proper steps are taken, you may be able to reduce the complications associated with the emergency and in so doing save your cat's life.

4

General Aid Techniques

Wounds and fractures accompany most injuries, especially traumatic ones. Since wounds may become infected quickly, it is important to know how to clean and bandage them, even before you arrive at the emergency clinic. If possible, fractures should be splinted to reduce swelling and lessen the chances of further injury during transport.

This chapter covers wounds and wound care, including how to apply specific bandages in different emergency situations and how to care for abscesses. A description of the different classes of fractures is provided as well as how to recognize and treat fractures. Finally, dislocations, sprains, and strains are defined, and the first aid for these conditions is discussed.

SECTION 1: WOUNDS

The two basic classes of wounds are *closed* (when the skin is not broken) and *open* (when the skin is broken). This section describes and illustrates general wound care and then discusses the many different types of open wounds that exist and specific first aid where it is pertinent.

Closed Wounds

A closed wound is also known as a bruise or contusion. It may occur in mild trauma and alongside open wounds in severe trauma. The signs include:

1. Swelling
2. Pain
3. Discoloration of the injured area due to bleeding under the skin

FIRST AID

- Within a few hours of the injury, apply cool compresses (*not ice*) to the wound.
- After 24 hours, use warm compresses.
- Look for signs of other injuries, especially if your cat was hit by a car.

Open Wounds

In open wounds, underlying tissues may be exposed since the skin has been broken. The types of open wounds you are likely to encounter are described and illustrated in Figure 4-1. *These wounds must be treated immediately to avoid infection, preferably within the first 6 hours.* If a wound becomes infected, you should call your veterinarian immediately. You will see the following signs when a wound is infected:

1. Pain, redness, swelling, and warmth at the wound site
2. Lameness if the infection is on the leg
3. Pus draining from the wound or collected under the bandage
4. Abscess formation if the infection occurs in a puncture wound (see discussion of abscesses below)
5. Fever, weakness, and decreased appetite

While nearly all types of open wounds may be treated by following the first aid procedures discussed below, some types require additional methods. Specific first aid procedures for abscesses and splinters are also listed below.

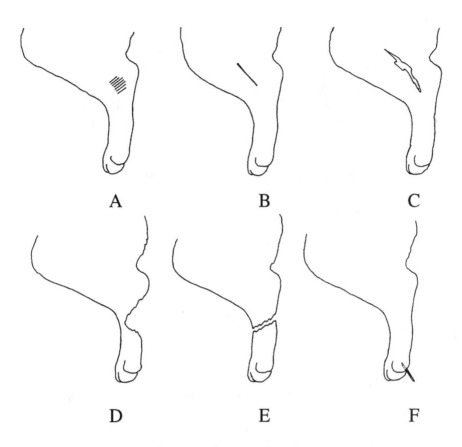

A   B   C

D   E   F

Figure 4-1: **(a) Abrasion.** An abrasion occurs when the skin is scraped by a hard surface; little bleeding is observed. **(b) Incision.** A cut from a sharp object with smooth, straight edges (such as a piece of broken glass, razor blade, or knife) can cause an incision. Heavy bleeding may be present along with possible damage to nerves and muscles. **(c) Laceration.** A laceration occurs when the skin is cut by an object with irregular sharp edges. A bite wound is a good example of a laceration. The tissue damage can be very great. **(d) Avulsion.** Avulsions occur when a body part is torn from the body but not completely separated, as may occur in wounds from traps and automobile accidents. **(e) Amputation.** Amputations occur when a body part, usually a leg, is severed from the rest of the body, as with lawn mower and chain saw accidents. **(f) Puncture.** Pointed objects such as teeth, claws, and splinters can cause puncture wounds. Because these wounds are difficult to clean, infections may easily occur.

FIRST AID

With severe bleeding

- *Stop* the bleeding (see Chapter 1, Section 6).
- *Bandage* the wound (see Section 2 of this chapter). Remember to incorporate the blood-soaked pad into the bandage, as removing the pad would disturb clot formation. Do not attempt to wash the wound.
- To bandage an amputation, include the severed part in the bandage in its normal position.
- Treat for shock (see Chapter 1, Section 6).

Without severe bleeding

- Wash your hands.
- Put first-aid materials on a clean blanket or towel within easy reach.
- Do not cough or breathe over the wound and do not touch it unless necessary.
- If you are using sterile pads or dressings, handle only the edges.
- Use tweezers to remove gravel and splinters from the wound itself (see Figure 4-2 [top left]).
- If mud or blood-soaked hair is on the skin surrounding the wound, attempt to remove it by wetting it or by combing it away from the wound (see Figure 4-2 [top right]).
- Using scissors that have been lubricated with petroleum jelly on the blades, clip the hair surrounding the wound (see Figure 4-2 [middle left]).
- Clean the skin surrounding the wound with soap and warm water. Use cotton balls or a washcloth and clean away from the wound (see Figure 4-2 [middle right]).
- Use a water pik or plenty of cool, clean water poured from a bottle or cup to clean the wound (see Figure 4-2 [bottom]). Use only water; do not use soap, detergent, or hydrogen peroxide.
- Bandage the wound (see Section 2).

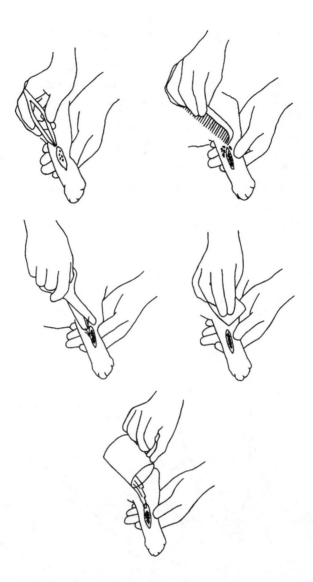

Figure 4-2: Top left: Removing gravel from the wound with tweezers. **Top right:** Combing mud or blood out of the fur surrounding the wound. Comb away from the wound. **Middle left:** Clipping the hair surrounding the wound with scissors. **Middle right:** Use a clean cloth with soap and water to clean the skin surrounding the wound. Clean from the edge of the wound outward. **Bottom:** To clean the wound itself, pour plenty of fresh, cool water over it.

- *Wash* the skin surface with mild soap and water.
- *Sterilize* tweezers by boiling for 5 minutes or heating the tips over a flame. Wipe off the black carbon coating with a sterile pad.
- *Remove* the splinter (see Figure 4-3).
- Once the splinter is removed, wash the area again with soap and water.
- If the splinter breaks or is too deeply lodged to remove, cover it with a sterile pad or clean cloth and wrap it lightly with adhesive tape. Have your veterinarian remove it as soon as possible.

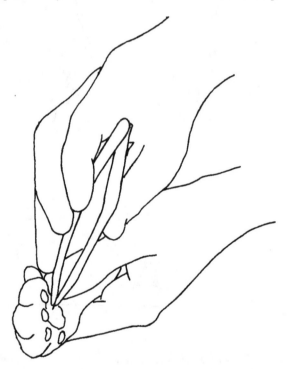

Figure 4-3: To remove a splinter, first loosen the skin surrounding the splinter with the end of the tweezers and then pull the splinter straight out.

Abscess

An abscess occurs when pus accumulates in a cavity or inside a sealed wound. Puncture wounds due to bites or claws from cats or other animals will often seal over before you have ever seen them. You will see the following signs in approximately two to five days:

1. Soft, fluctuant swelling in the area of the original wound
2. Lameness if the infection is on the leg
3. Possibly a decreased appetite
4. Possibly a fever

FIRST AID

- Take your cat to the veterinarian so the abscess can be lanced and drained.
- If the abscess has opened *on its own*, clean the wound as described above and apply warm packs for 10 minutes at a time, twice a day for 1 week. This will keep the abscess from forming again and will promote healing. Check with your veterinarian to see if the cat needs antibiotics.

Nonhealing Wounds

If you are treating a wound and it does not seem to be healing well, you should bring the cat to a veterinarian to be examined. Some reasons the wound may not be healing include chronic virus infections (e.g., feline leukemia virus or feline immunodeficiency virus) or the presence of a foreign body or fly larva such as *Cuterebra* under the skin.

Cats become exposed to the *Cuterebra* fly by being outside and near rodent burrows in the summertime. The larva will migrate under the skin of the neck and chest; as it grows under the skin, it creates an abscess. The signs are:

1. A thick-walled abscess just under the skin
2. Constant licking of the neck or chest
3. Possibly pus
4. Possibly a tiny breathing hole through the skin

There is no first aid as such except to recognize the signs and bring your cat to the veterinarian to have the larva removed and abscess cleaned. *Do not squeeze the abscess area* in an attempt to remove the larva, as you may rupture the larva and cause anaphylaxis (see Chapter 3, Section 1).

SECTION 2: BANDAGING

This section emphasizes proper bandaging technique. I will first describe and illustrate the three main parts of a bandage and then show how to bandage specific parts of the body for the most common emergencies. How to keep the bandage on your cat (including the use of an Elizabethan collar) is discussed.

There are four good reasons to bandage a wound:

1. To keep the wound from becoming more contaminated
2. To protect it from further trauma, including self-mutilation
3. To keep it moist
4. To absorb blood seeping from the wound

General Technique and Components

A simple bandage is made up of three layers: a pad, gauze, and adhesive tape. In certain bandages, other materials must be added; these are discussed below under specific bandages.

1. **Pad**   This is the first layer of the bandage and is the part which comes into direct contact with the wound. In general, *nonstick pads* are better as they will not disturb any healing that takes place. *Sterile pads* are

preferable to nonsterile pads, but most important, you should use something that is *absorbent, clean, and dust-free,* even if it is a washcloth or piece of towel. It is not necessary to put ointment on the pad before you place it over the wound. **Do not use petroleum jelly** because it is not water soluble and therefore is very difficult to clean off the wound. If you want to use an ointment, use Neosporin® or Bacitracin. Never put ointment on the pad when bandaging deep wounds, open fractures, or burns, because these wounds are extremely difficult to clean once ointment has been applied. Place the pad over the cleaned wound (see Section 1, "Wounds," and Figure 4-4 [top]).

2. **Gauze** The middle layer is made of gauze. I do not advise using elastic or stretch gauze. Although it is easier to apply, it is also easier to wrap too tightly, increasing the chances of cutting off the circulation, causing swelling and cool, bluish-colored skin. Roll the gauze over the pad so it is secure but not too tight (see Figure 4-4 [bottom left]). As you roll, you should try to overlap the gauze by about one third.

3. **Adhesive Tape** The outer layer consists of adhesive tape, which holds the bandage down. Elastic adhesive may cause the same problem as elastic gauze. The adhesive tape should be applied in the same manner as the gauze, catching bits of hair at the top edge and bottom edge of the bandage. To ensure that the bandage was not put on too tightly, you should always be able to fit two fingers between the bandage and the skin (see Figure 4-4 [bottom right]). This must be done for all bandages you apply. The bandage should be changed daily unless your veterinarian advises otherwise.

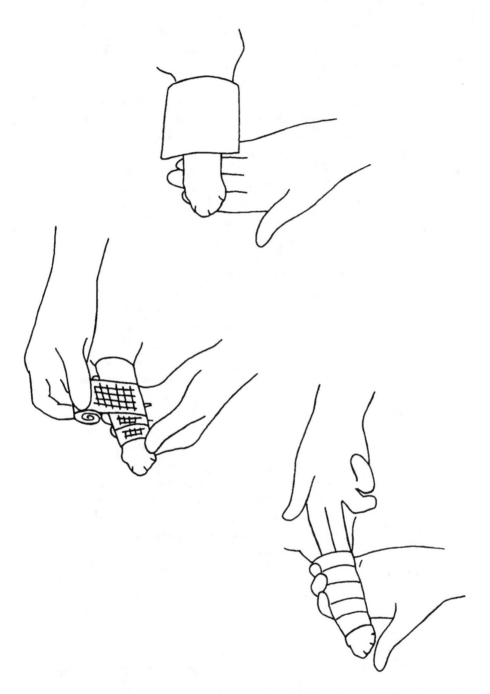

Figure 4-4: Top: Place the pad over the cleaned wound. **Bottom left:** Wrap the gauze over the pad. **Bottom right:** Wrap the adhesive tape over the gauze. Two fingers should be able to fit between the bandage and the skin.

Bandages for Specific Areas

1. **Eye**   For eye injuries involving nonpenetrating foreign objects, trauma to the eye surface and lids, and prolapse of the eye.

Figure 4-5: Top left: Place a pad over the affected eye (NOTE: the pad should be moistened with sterile saline or cool water before being placed against a prolapsed eye). Gauze is wrapped over the pad, starting at the top of the head in front of the ear opposite the affected eye. **Top right:** The gauze is continued under the chin and around the head, this time going behind the ear opposite the affected eye. Continue wrapping, alternating the gauze in front of and behind the ear opposite the affected eye. **Bottom:** Cover the gauze with adhesive tape in the same manner as the gauze was applied.

109

2. **Ear**   For wounds to the ear.

Figure 4-6: Top left: Place a pad against the cleaned wound. **Top right:** Mold a piece of cotton to fit into the ear. **Bottom:** Secure the molded cotton with short strips of adhesive tape going from the edge of the ear across the cotton to the other edge. When the bandage is finished, the cotton should be completely covered with the tape.

3. Neck   For any wounds to the neck.

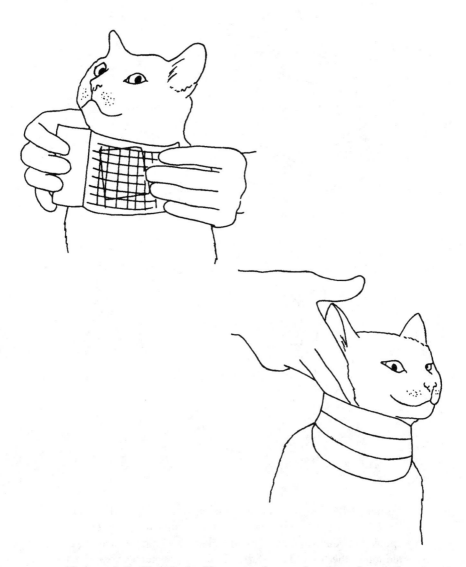

Figure 4-7: Top Left: Place a pad over the cleaned wound and wrap gauze over the pad with as *little tension* as possible. **Bottom Right:** Cover the gauze with adhesive tape making sure that two fingers can fit easily between the bandage and the neck. Your cat should not have any difficulty breathing while the bandage is on.

4. **Chest/** For any wounds of the chest or abdomen.
   Abdomen

Figure 4-8: Top left: Place a pad against the wound (*NOTE:* For chest wounds, wet the pad with sterile saline or cool water and apply at the end of an exhalation) and cover with gauze starting at the top of the back. **Top right:** To make sure the gauze doesn't slip backward, wrap the gauze around the trunk alternating in front of and behind the foreleg on the same side as the wound. **Bottom:** Cover the gauze with adhesive tape in the same manner as the gauze was applied. To keep the bandage more secure, catch a small amount of fur at the edges of the bandage. Be sure that two fingers can fit between the bandage and the skin and that your cat can breathe easily while the bandage is in place.

5. **Rump**   For all wounds of the rump.

Figure 4-9: Top left: Apply a pad over the cleaned wound. Starting at midabdomen, wrap gauze up the left side to the back and down the right side of the abdomen. Run the gauze through the legs, staying to the left side of the tail. **Top right:** Circle the trunk by going down the right side and up the left side. Then bring the gauze over to the right side of the tail and through the legs to the left flank. Repeat this crisscross pattern at least twice. **Bottom:** Cover the gauze with adhesive tape, catching some fur on the edges and applying in the same crisscross pattern as the gauze. Your cat should be able to walk, urinate, and defecate normally with the bandage on. If you have a male cat, you may have to cut an opening in the bandage for the cat's penis.

6. **Leg**   For any wound of the leg when you *don't* suspect a fracture.

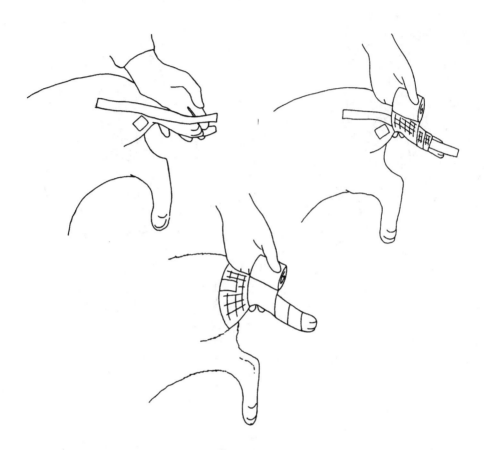

Figure 4-10: Top left: Place a pad over the cleaned wound. Place two strips of adhesive tape along the side surfaces of the leg, extending approximately 4 to 5 inches above and below the wound if possible. Place the strips so you avoid the wound, even if that means using only one strip. **Top right:** Gauze is wrapped around the leg starting at the lower end with evenly applied pressure, leaving approximately 1 inch of adhesive tape exposed at the top and bottom. **Bottom:** Turn the exposed strips of adhesive tape onto the gauze so that the sticky side is up. Wrap adhesive tape in the same manner as the gauze, catching some fur at the edges. *For full leg bandages,* leave several toes visible so that you can check to see if the bandage is on too tight. A bandage that is too tight will result in swollen, blue, or cold toes. You should be able easily to insert two fingers between the bandage and the skin.

7. **Foot**   For wounds on the foot.

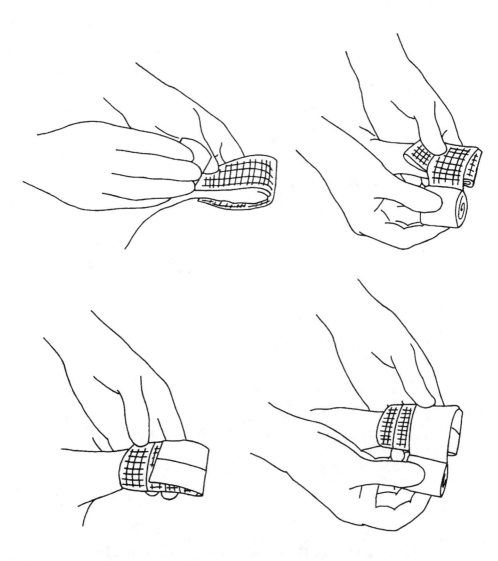

Figure 4-11: Top left: Place a pad over the cleaned wound. Use gauze folded back on itself to cover the very bottom of the paw. **Top right:** With even pressure, wrap gauze around the paw from the bottom up to cover the layers of folded gauze. **Bottom left:** Cover the bottom of the paw with strips of adhesive tape. **Bottom right:** Wrap the adhesive tape around the foot in the same manner as the gauze. To secure the bandage, catch some fur on the top edge.

8. **Tail**   For wounds on the tail.

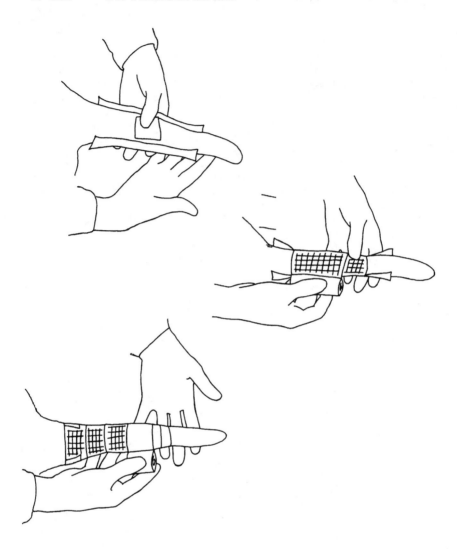

Figure 4-12: Top: Place a pad over the cleaned wound. Place two strips of adhesive tape on the tail, avoiding the wound. Extend the tape approximately 3 to 4 inches *above and below* the wound if possible. **Middle:** Wrap the gauze with even pressure around the tail, starting at the bottom and leaving approximately one inch of tape exposed at the top and bottom. **Bottom:** Turn the exposed adhesive strips back onto the gauze and wrap adhesive tape around the tail, starting at the end of the reflected strip and at the bottom of the tail.

Elizabethan Collar

No matter how securely you apply a bandage, chances are your cat will be able to remove it if given enough time. The use of an Elizabethan collar (see Figure 4-13) will slow the process down considerably and should prevent the cat from bothering the bandages altogether. Elizabethan collars can be used to protect head bandages as well as bandages anywhere else on the body.

Your veterinarian can supply you with an Elizabethan collar. However, if you need one in an emergency (e.g., penetrating foreign object in the eye), you can easily make one as follows:

- Measure the diameter of your cat's body at the largest point. This will usually be from shoulder to shoulder.
- Cut a circular piece of cardboard half again (1½ times) the measured diameter. Use light cardboard (for example, from a gift box), if possible. If not, use the thinnest box cardboard you can find.
- Cut a hole in the center large enough to fit your cat's neck plus two fingers.
- Cut the collar on one side, from the center hole to the outer edge. Fit your cat's head into it and then tape over the cut with masking or adhesive tape.

Figure 4-13: Elizabethan collar. See text for instructions on how to make one.

After you put on the collar, stay and watch the cat's reaction. If she doesn't seem to adjust after a short time or becomes very nervous and tries to tear it off, you should remove the collar. If you decide to leave the collar on, make sure that your cat can eat and drink normally while wearing it.

117

SECTION 3: FRACTURES

Fractures usually occur when your cat has been hit by a car or has been sub-
jected to some other form of severe trauma, such as falling or jumping from a
high location. This section will describe and illustrate two major classifica-
tions of fractures and then discuss the signs and first aid for three types of
fractures: spinal, pelvic, and leg.

Kinds of Fractures

An **open fracture** has a break in the skin caused by the bone (see Figure
4-14 [top left]). A **closed fracture** has no break in the skin (see Figure
4-14 [top right]).

A **simple fracture** involves a bone broken into two pieces (Figure 4-14
[bottom left]). A **comminuted fracture** has bone broken into *more than two*
pieces (see Figure 4-14 [bottom right]).

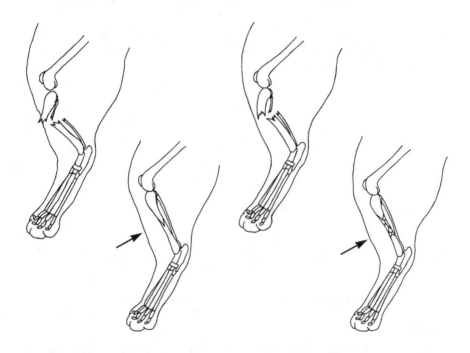

Figure 4-14: Top left: Open fracture. **Top right:** Closed fracture. **Bottom left:** Simple fracture. **Bottom right:** Comminuted
fracture.

General Signs of Fracture and First Aid

Although the signs of a fracture will very much depend on its type, severity, and location (see below), you may see the following signs with any type of fracture:

1. Swelling
2. Hot or cold skin temperature
3. Bluish color to the skin
4. Lameness

When considering first aid for fractures, it is important to remember that if a cat just suffered severe trauma, such as being hit by a car, there may be other more serious problems. Shock, bleeding, or difficulty breathing need to be treated *before* the fracture (see Chapter 1, Section 1, "Triage"). The signs and first aid for specific fractures are given below.

The signs seen with **spinal fractures** will greatly depend on which part of the spinal cord is injured. In general, the signs are:

1. Paralysis (inability to move or feel pain) in legs or tail
2. Weakness in the legs

FIRST AID

- The first aid for spinal fractures is *proper transport* so as not to increase injury to the spinal cord (see Chapter 1, Section 2, "Transporting a Cat with Spinal Cord Injuries," and Figure 1-8).
- Treat for shock as needed (see Chapter 1, Section 6).

A cat with a **pelvic fracture** will be able to move the front legs normally but will be either unable to move the back legs or will try to stand up only to have the back legs immediately go out sideways. Often, leg fractures and severe internal injuries will accompany a pelvic fracture. Due to pain in the pelvic area, your cat may not be willing to defecate or urinate.

FIRST AID

- If your cat is unable to move her back legs, treat just as you would a spinal fracture.
- If your cat attempts to stand up, you can help by using a towel sling (see Figure 4-15).

119

Figure 4-15: Towel sling. Fold a soft bath towel into halves or thirds lengthwise. Center the towel under your cat's abdomen and pull up on the two ends to make a sling.

The major sign of a **leg fracture** is that your cat will not want to bear weight on the injured leg, although you should keep in mind that some cats do not know this rule. If your cat is limping on one leg, it doesn't necessarily mean that she has a fractured leg, and if the cat walks on the leg, it doesn't mean that the leg is not broken.

FIRST AID

- If you suspect a leg fracture, apply a temporary splint before moving your cat. If your cat becomes too stressed, stop and transport her directly to your veterinarian as shown in Figure 1-8.
- You may use a hand towel or a heavily padded bandage as a temporary splint. For added support, incorporate into the splint a tongue depressor or piece of heavy cardboard cut to the shape of the leg. For a towel splint, see Figure 3-2 [bottom].
- For the best stability, the splint should cover the joint above and the joint below the suspected fracture.
- A heavily padded bandage provides the best support for a leg fracture (see Figure 4-16). If the fracture is open, apply a pad over the unwashed wound. *Do not put ointment on the pad.*

- After the fracture is immobilized, check the cat from head to toe on the way to the veterinarian, as the animal may have suffered other injuries that you cannot see.
- When your cat has a fracture:

   (a) **Never** try to **manipulate** the bones back into their normal place.
   (b) **Never wash out** fractures.
   (c) Apply a temporary splint, if possible. If not possible, transport, as shown in Figure 1-8, to a veterinarian.

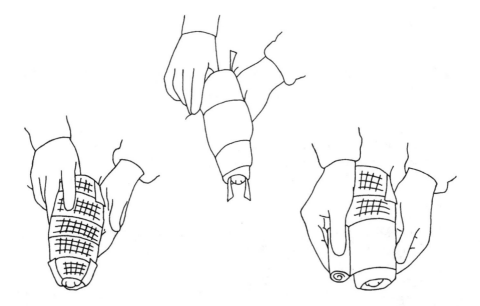

Figure 4-16: Top: To make a heavily padded bandage splint, absorbent cotton or a clean hand towel is rolled tightly around the limb after adhesive tape strips have been applied, as in Figure 4-10. Start wrapping the cotton or towel at the foot and move up. Leave one to two toes visible so that you can check to see if the bandage has been put on too tightly (swollen, blue, or cold toes). **Bottom left:** Roll the gauze tightly down on the towel, starting at the paw and working up to the whole length of the leg. The strips of adhesive tape are then turned back so that the sticky side is up. **Bottom right:** The adhesive tape is applied with tension over the gauze, starting at the foot and working up. Remember to leave several toes visible.

SECTION 4: DISLOCATIONS, SPRAINS, AND STRAINS

Dislocations, sprains, and strains may all produce the same general signs as fractures, and because of this, they are usually treated in the same manner until a fracture is ruled out. A *dislocation* occurs when a bone pops out of its joint, usually due to severe trauma. *Sprains* are torn or stretched ligaments, tendons, and blood vessels around joints and are also caused by severe trauma. *Strains* are torn or stretched muscles around joints. They are caused by sudden physical exertion.

All of these conditions may produce the following signs:

1. Painful joints
2. Swollen joints
3. Discoloration
4. Lameness

FIRST AID

- If your cat is limping, apply a temporary splint if possible (see Figures 3-2 [bottom] and 4-16).
- If your cat is not limping and the trauma occurred within the past few hours, confine your cat and apply cool compresses to the joint. If the trauma occurred more than 24 hours ago, apply warm compresses.
- In either situation, have your veterinarian examine the cat *soon* to determine the true problem.

SUMMARY

Because nearly all cats suffer wounds at some point in their lives, you should know how to treat an abscess, dress a wound, and apply a proper bandage. In severe trauma, such as occurs in auto accidents and falls, wounds may be complicated by fractures, dislocations, and sprains. Recognizing the relevant signs, you can transport your cat in a way that will minimize the pain and complications due to the fracture.

5

Emergency Situations:
Sample Cases, Problem Sets

T he following cases are taken from real-life emergency situations. Read them through carefully and then decide what you would do. The answers are given in Appendix 3.

CASE 1:

You are just settling down for the evening after a hard day. In walks Snowball, your three-year-old white Domestic Shorthair, who is coughing and wheezing. You are not too alarmed because Snowball has been diagnosed by your veterinarian as having asthma. But this time, Snowball starts gasping for air. In a matter of minutes, she has progressed to open-mouth breathing and the color of her gums is now approaching faint blue. You call the vet. He tells you to bring her in immediately. Before you can get her into the car, Snowball stops breathing.

CASE 2:

It is getting late and there is still no sign of Wanda, your one-year-old Domestic Shorthair. You know Wanda is never late for dinner, so you walk down to the road. After walking a few yards, you spot Wanda in a heap on the side of the road. When she sees you, she tries to get up but can only lift her upper body. On closer inspection, you notice a large gash over her hind end and a piece of bone protruding from her right hind leg. She is breathing rapidly and the color of her gums is quite pale.

CASE 3:

You plan to run into the bank, where cats are not allowed, to make a deposit. It is a hot day, so you park in the shade and leave your window cracked so Pooh Bear, your twelve-year-old Himalayan, can have some fresh air. In the bank, you chat with a friend you haven't seen for years. By the time you return to your car, Pooh Bear is collapsed on the backseat. You evaluate the situation and find your cat feels extremely hot and is not breathing but has a pulse.

CASE 4:

Your three-year-old Domestic Longhair, Charlemagne, comes back from a night excursion in the woods with some matted fur and dried blood on his left front leg. After examining the cat, you find several bite wounds. You clean the wounds and bring the cat to your veterinarian for a thorough check. Except for the bite wounds, Charlemagne is declared normal. Your veterinarian prescribes antibiotics to prevent the bite wounds from becoming infected. Later that day, as you are walking through the woods behind your house, you spot a dead raccoon with porcupine quills covering its head and mouth.

CASE 5:

You have noticed that Sambo, your ten-year-old neutered Siamese, has not been himself lately. He hasn't eaten much since yesterday and today seems to constantly be in the litterbox. You observe him in the litterbox and note that he seems to be straining to urinate but is not producing any urine.

CASE 6:

You are traveling on the road with Leo, your ten-year-old Domestic Shorthair. Since you still have a few hours' driving time until you reach your destination, you decide to take a stretch at the next rest stop. You have brought a harness and leash and put them on Leo before taking him out of the car. You have just started to walk around when a large dog approaches and lunges for Leo. Before you can pick Leo up, the dog has grabbed him and shaken him a few times. You bring Leo to your car to examine him. He is dazed, breathing with difficulty, and has numerous puncture wounds on the chest and abdomen. His gums are pale, and his pulse is weak.

Appendix:
How to Prevent Emergencies

Call Your Veterinarian
In any emergency, even when you have already provided first aid, notify your veterinarian and have your cat examined. Even in the case of a minor accident, you may have overlooked serious problems.

Electrical Hazards
All electrical wires should be safely stored away and out of sight of your cat. Out of boredom or playfulness, cats, especially kittens, may chew on the wires and get a serious burn in the mouth. *Always remember to unplug the cord before giving first aid.*

Examinations
Make sure your cat is examined once a year by your veterinarian. Catch problems before they start.

Food
Never feed your cat table food, as it is usually too high in fat. Feed commercial food or a homemade diet approved by your veterinarian. Always provide plenty of fresh water.

Poisons

Keep your cleaners, polishers, bleaches, and detergents high up or under the sink in a *locked* cabinet. Many common household chemicals may cause your cat to become sick (see Table 3-2).

Houseplants should be kept high up and out of the way of your cat. Many plants can make your cat sick, and some may even cause severe illness or death (see Table 3-3).

Keep your cat's medicines, as well as your own, high up or in a locked cabinet. *Never* give medications to your cat without first checking with your veterinarian.

Trash

Keep your garbage secure both inside and outside your house.

Traveling

When traveling with your cat, be sure to use a carrier or box that is secured in your car. As an extra precaution, never leave car windows down far enough so that the cat could get out. *Do not* confine your cat in a car while running errands, shopping, and so on.

Weather

During the summer, make sure your cat has access to shade, fresh air, and cool water. Avoid leaving the animal in an unventilated space, for example, a parked car or house that is not air-conditioned with windows closed. When the windows are open, *be sure screens are in place*, as the cat might fall out accidentally while playing or sleeping on the sill. If you use window fans, make sure that they have protective shields to prevent a cat's foot or tail from becoming caught in the fan blades.

Appendix:
Drug Dosages

MEDICATIONS

Oral medications may be given in liquid form or in pill form.

When giving **liquid medicine,** administer it with a plastic medicine dropper. These droppers are calibrated in teaspoons/milliliters and can be purchased in a pharmacy. Give the medicine in an even movement with the dropper pointed toward the base of the tongue, not up at the roof of the mouth (see Figure A-1 [top]).

When giving **a pill,** first try to hide it inside a little bit of canned food or peanut butter, then offer it to your cat. This method works best with small pills. If this doesn't work, give the pill as shown in Figure A-1 [bottom], holding the cat's mouth open and dropping the pill toward the back of the mouth. To make it easier to swallow the pill, smear it with a small amount of honey or butter. Once you have dropped the pill into the cat's mouth, close the mouth and rub the throat to encourage swallowing. If your cat is still not cooperating, try putting a little canned food in his mouth, and hopefully the pill, which was thrown in earlier, will get swallowed with the food!

Never give oral medication to a cat who is vomiting, unconscious, choking, or gagging. Always check with your veterinarian before giving any medications.

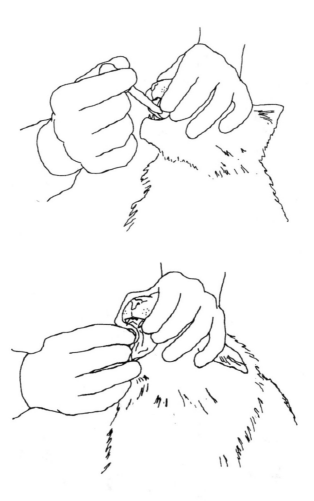

Figure A-1: Top: To give liquid medication with a medicine dropper, hold the cat's upper jaw with one hand, placing your thumb on one side and the rest of your fingers on the other side. The other hand holds the medicine dropper. Point the dropper toward the bottom of the mouth and give the medicine slowly and evenly. **Bottom:** To give your cat a pill, hold the upper jaw with one hand, placing your thumb on one side and the rest of your fingers on the other side. Tilt the cat's head back until the nose points upward; this will help the lower jaw to open slightly. Gently press on the lower jaw with the middle finger of your other hand, and holding the pill between your thumb and index finger, drop it toward the back of the cat's mouth.

Antibiotic Ointment
- Reduces the chance of infection if used on a pad as part of a bandage (see Chapter 4, Section 2).
- Use Neosporin® or Bacitracin.

Activated Charcoal
- Absorbs small amounts of poison. Works best after vomiting has occurred.
- Dosage: 0.5 gram of charcoal per pound of the cat's body weight. To make a slurry (liquid paste) from the powder form or tablets that have been ground, mix each gram of charcoal with 1 to 2 teaspoons of water. This will mix up to a consistency you can administer with a medicine dropper. Give this by mouth once.

Hydrogen peroxide (3 percent)
- Induces vomiting.
- Dosage: 1 teaspoon by mouth. If vomiting does not occur within 15 minutes, repeat once.

Syrup of Ipecac
- Induces vomiting.
- Dosage: Give 1 to 2 teaspoons once by mouth.

Vegetable Oil, Mineral Oil
- Coats the intestine and helps pass poisons through the gastro-intestinal tract.
- Dosage: Give 1 to 2 teaspoons once by mouth.

3
Appendix:
Answers to Problem Sets

CASE 1:

Snowball is suffering from asthma (see Chapter 3, Section 2) and is probably having an attack. Because she has stopped breathing, you should start CPR immediately (see Chapter 1, Section 3, and Figure 1-11). If possible, have someone drive while you perform CPR on the way to the hospital. Remember to open the airway and check for any obstructions before beginning artificial respiration (see Figure 1-12). Even though it is most likely that Snowball is having an asthma attack, the signs may also indicate an obstruction in the mouth or throat.

CASE 2:

Wanda has probably been hit by a car and now is in shock (see Chapter 1, Section 6). Her breathing difficulties may indicate that she has internal injuries as well as the wounds and open fracture that you can see.

Since Wanda is off the road, you can begin treatment. Start by gently sliding the cat onto your coat and wrapping it over her, since pale gums and rapid respiration indicate that she is probably in shock. Apply pressure to any wounds that are bleeding severely and then bandage. It is best not to transport Wanda until you have splinted the fracture (see Chapter 4, Section 3) and can move her on something firm, as there may be a spinal cord injury (see Chapter 1, Section 2). Remember not to wash the open fracture site. Call ahead before taking Wanda in to see your veterinarian. If possible, monitor breathing and pulse on the way.

CASE 3:

Pooh Bear is probably suffering from heat stroke. Even though you parked in the shade, there was not enough fresh, moving air to counteract the effect of the heat. First, move the cat out of the car into a shady, ventilated area and then begin CPR (see Chapter 1, Section 3). If someone is present who can help, have her or him call your veterinarian and drive you there while you continue CPR. If Pooh Bear starts breathing before being seen by your vet, be sure to take his temperature and give ice baths if necessary (see Chapter 3, Section 11). Monitor his temperature, pulse, and respirations until he can be seen.

CASE 4:

Because Charlemagne may have been bitten by the raccoon that you have just found, you should be concerned about rabies (see Chapter 3, Section 4). The porcupine quills on the face of the raccoon indicate that the raccoon was not behaving normally, possibly due to rabies.

You should notify the local health department of the situation. The raccoon will have to be tested for rabies. If the rabies test is positive, you will be advised to receive postexposure shots *even if* you have received preexposure vaccinations.

You should call your veterinarian and check to see if the rabies vaccination for your cat is up to date or check the rabies certificate that you received at the time the cat was vaccinated. If Charlemagne's rabies vaccination is up to date, he should receive a booster rabies shot. If not, the cat will have to be quarantined for a period of time at your expense or be euthanized.

CASE 5:

Sambo most likely has a blockage in the urinary tract (see Chapter 3, Section 13). You should call your veterinarian immediately, because Sambo is at risk of becoming dehydrated and going into shock over a short period of time.

CASE 6:

Leo's pale gums and weak pulse indicate shock (see Chapter 1, Section 6). The fact that he is breathing with difficulty may mean that the bite wounds suffered extend all the way into the chest cavity. You should treat for shock by keeping him covered and quiet. Stop severe bleeding and if possible apply moist bandages to the chest wounds (see Chapter 2, Section 5, and Chapter 4, Figure 4-8). If abdominal organs are protruding from any bite wounds, do not attempt to push them back into the abdominal cavity; instead, place a moist cloth or gauze pad over them and bandage this area (see Chapter 2, Section 6, and Chapter 4, Figure 4-8). Remember not to wash wounds that you believe extend into the chest or abdominal cavities. You should find the nearest veterinary clinic and have Leo seen immediately. Continue to treat for shock and monitor pulse and respiration.

Bibliography

American Red Cross. *American Red Cross Standard First Aid Workbook.* Washington, DC: American National Red Cross, 1988.

Appel, Max J. G. "Lyme Disease in Dogs and Cats." *Compendium for Continuing Education*: Vol. 12, No. 5 (May 1990): 617–626.

Behler, John L., and King, F. Wayne. *The Audubon Society Field Guide to North American Reptiles and Amphibians.* New York: Alfred A. Knopf, 1979.

"Curiosity Can Kill the Cat." *Perspectives On Cats* (Cornell Feline Health Center Newsletter): Summer 1992: 1.

DeCamp, Charles E. "Principles of Pelvic Fracture Management." *Veterinary Medicine and Surgery (Small Animal)*: Vol. 7, No. 1 (Feb. 1992): 63–70.

Dye, Janice A. "Feline Bronchopulmonary Disease." *Veterinary Clinics of North America, Small Animal Practice*: Vol. 22, No. 5 (Sept. 1992): 1187–1201.

Ettinger, Stephen J. (ed.). *Textbook of Veterinary Internal Medicine: Diseases of the Dog and Cat, Third Edition*: Vols. 1 and 2. Philadelphia: W.B. Saunders Co., 1989.

Fowler, Murray E. *Plant Poisoning in Small Companion Animals.* St. Louis: Ralston Purina, Co., 1980.

Fraser, Clarence M. (ed.). *The Merck Veterinary Manual*, Sixth Edition. Rahway: Merck & Co., 1986.

Holzworth, Jean. *Diseases of the Cat*: Vol. 1. Philadelphia: W.B. Saunders Co., 1987.

Kirk, Robert W. (ed.). *Current Veterinary Therapy, VIII*. Philadelphia: W.B. Saunders Co., 1983.

Kirk, Robert W., Bistner, Stephen I., and Ford, R. B. (eds.). *Handbook of Veterinary Procedures and Emergency Treatment*. Philadelphia: W.B. Saunders Co., 1990.

Knecht, Charles D. *Fundamental Techniques in Veterinary Surgery*. Philadelphia: W.B. Saunders Co., 1981.

Leighton, Robert L. "Principles of Conservative Fracture Management: Splints and Casts." *Seminars in Veterinary Medicine and Surgery (Small Animal)*: Vol. 6, No. 1 (Feb. 1991): 39–51.

"Lyme Disease in Cats." *Perspectives On Cats* (Cornell Feline Health Center Newsletter): Spring 1992: 3.

Moses, Bradley L., and Spaulding, Glen L. "Chronic Bronchial Disease of the Cat." *Veterinary Clinics of North America, Small Animal Practice*: Vol. 15, No. 15 (Sept. 1985): 929–948.

Muller, George H. *Small Animal Dermatology*. Philadelphia: W.B. Saunders Co., 1983.

Oliver, J. E., and Lorenz, M. D. *Handbook of Veterinary Neurology*. Philadelphia: W.B. Saunders Co., 1993.

Osborne, Carl A., et al. "Feline Urologic Signs: Hypothesis of Heterogeneous Causes." *Veterinary Previews*: Issue 1, No. 1 (1994): 2–18.

Plunkett, Signe. *Emergency Procedures for the Small Animal Veterinarian*. Philadelphia: W.B. Saunders Co., 1993.

Proceedings of the Third International Veterinary Emergency and Critical Care Symposium. September 20–23, 1992. San Antonio: Veterinary Emergency and Critical Care Society, 1992.

Stamp, Gary L. (ed.). Veterinary Clinics of North America, Small Animal Practice: Vol. 19, No. 6 (1989).

Slatter, D. H. *Fundamentals of Veterinary Opthalmology*. Philadelphia: W.B. Saunders Co., 1990.

Zaslow, Ira M. (ed.). *Veterinary Trauma and Critical Care*. Philadelphia: Lea & Febiger, 1984.

Glossary

Abrasion: a type of wound that occurs when the skin is scraped by a hard surface.

Abscess: an accumulation of pus in a cavity or inside a sealed wound.

Airway: the path by which air enters the body and flows to and from the lungs.

Ambulatory: able to walk.

Amputation: the severance of a body part, usually a leg, from the rest of the body.

Anaphylactic shock: a type of allergic reaction that occurs within a few minutes.

Anemia: a reduction in the number of red blood cells or hemoglobin in the blood, causing weakness.

Antivenom: a remedy used in the treatment of animal venom bites or stings, containing specific venom-neutralizing substances.

Artery: a vessel that carries blood from the heart to different parts of the body.

Artificial respiration: a type of rescue breathing where air is forced from the mouth of the rescuer into the nose and lungs of the victim.

Asthma: a condition characterized by recurrent attacks of difficult or labored breathing.

Avulsion: a tearing of a body part from the rest of the body without complete separation.

Bronchi: the larger air passages that lead from the trachea to the lungs.

Capillary refill time: the time it takes the tiny blood vessels under the skin to refill once they have been emptied by manual pressure.

Cardiopulmonary failure: an absence of normal heart and lung function.

Cardiopulmonary resuscitation: a technique that combines artificial respiration and chest compressions in cases where the heart and lungs cease to function.

Chest cavity: the space within the upper part of the body that contains the lungs.

Circulation: the flow of blood through the body. Circulation may be assessed by checking the pulse, color of the gums, and capillary refill time.

Closed fracture: a broken bone not accompanied by a break in the skin.

Closed wound: a wound where the skin is not broken; also known as a bruise or contusion.

Coma: a complete loss of consciousness with no response to pain.

Comminuted fracture: a type of fracture in which the bone is broken into more than two pieces.

Constrict: to close down or become smaller.

Convulsions: involuntary contraction of muscles.

Cornea: the outer, visible layer of the eyeball.

Cuterebra: a type of fly whose larval stage lives under the skin and produces a nonhealing wound.

Cyanosis: a bluish discoloration of the skin or gums, resulting from inadequate oxygenation of the blood.

Dehydration: a condition that indicates loss of body water. Dehydration is commonly caused by vomiting and diarrhea and may lead to shock.

Dermis: the lower layer of the skin.

Devitalized: dead.

Diabetes: a disease wherein there occurs an overproduction of urine and a decreased effect of insulin on the body.

Dilate: to open up or become larger.

Dislocation: a condition that occurs when a bone comes out of its joint.

Distal: anatomically located far from the origin of attachment.

Eclampsia: muscle tremors that occur in the female cat after giving birth.

Electric shock: a condition resulting from contact of the body with an exposed wire.

Elizabethan collar: a type of collar that extends outward from the neck and is designed to prevent a cat from removing a bandage, licking a wound, or scratching certain areas.

Epidermis: the top layer of the skin.

Epilepsy: a disorder of the central nervous system characterized by *recurrent* seizures.

Exhale: to push air out of the lungs.

Finger sweep: a technique used to check the mouth of a choking cat.

First-degree burn: a burn that involves only the epidermis; also known as a superficial burn.

Fluctuant: appearing to contain liquid.

Fracture: a break in a bone.

Frostbite: the freezing of small areas of the body due to exposure to the cold.

Full thickness burn: a burn that involves the entire thickness of the skin; also known as a third-degree burn.

Gastritis: inflammation of the stomach.

Glaucoma: a condition resulting from increased pressure within the eye.

Grand mal seizure: a type of generalized seizure characterized by the presence of convulsions.

Hairball: an object made up of groomed hair and stomach contents; it may be passed through the digestive tract in a normal fashion or be vomited.

Head-to-toe exam: an evaluation of the major body systems to check for problems that are not obvious.

Heat stroke: an internal body temperature of 105°F or higher, usually resulting from confinement in hot weather.

Heimlich-like maneuver: an abdominal thrust performed just below the sternum or rib cage to help remove a foreign object lodged in the airway.

Hematoma: a swelling that contains blood; usually found on the ear.

Hemorrhage: severe bleeding.

Hives: a type of allergic reaction that takes from 20 minutes to 2 hours to develop and involves redness and swelling in the eyes and mouth.

Hypersensitive: an increased ability to show allergic symptoms when in contact with certain substances, such as vaccines or drugs.

Hypothermia: generalized body chilling due to exposure to the cold.

Idiopathic: having no known cause.

Incision: a type of wound that results from being cut by a sharp object with smooth, straight edges.

Infection: the invasion and multiplication of microorganisms in the body.

Inflammation: localized swelling, heat, redness, and pain as a result of injury, infection, or irritation.

Inflammatory Bowel Disease: a common cause of chronic vomiting and diarrhea in cats.

Inhale: to take air into the lungs.

Insidious condition: a problem that develops gradually and subtly.

Insulin: a substance used to lower blood sugar in the treatment of diabetes.

Intussusception: a condition that occurs when one part of the intestine pushes into the inside of another part.

Iris: the colored portion of the eye.

Laceration: a type of wound that occurs when the skin is cut by an object with sharp, irregular edges.

Ligament: the fibrous structure that connects one part of bone or cartilage to another.

Low-grade fever: an internal body temperature of 1 to 2 degrees above normal.

Obstruction: a blockage that may occur in the airway, gastrointestinal tract, urinary tract, or circulatory system.

Open fracture: a broken bone accompanied by a break in the skin.

Open wound: a type of wound in which the skin is broken.

Paralysis: the inability to move or feel pain.

Partial thickness burn: a type of burn that involves the entire epidermis and part of the dermis; also known as a second-degree burn.

Pressure point: a point where hand pressure is applied to the main artery supplying the bleeding area.

Prolapse: a condition that occurs when a body part slips out of its normal location, for example, eye or rectum.

Prostration: lying down full length.

Pulse: the throbbing of the heartbeat as felt in the major arteries. The pulse is commonly taken by lightly pressing in the groin, which is the location of the femoral artery.

Puncture wound: a type of wound that is caused by a pointed object, such as a tooth or claw.

Pupil: the opening at the center of the colored portion of the eye.

Rabies: a viral disease affecting the brain, usually transmitted by bite wounds, usually fatal once signs occur; all warm-blooded animals are susceptible.

Rectum: the end of the gastrointestinal tract, which opens out to the anus.

Respiration rate: the number of breaths taken per minute.

Responsive: the ability to react to a number of actions, such as calling, clapping, or touching.

Restraint: a technique of holding that allows the rescuer to give first aid safely.

Retinal detachment: the separation of the innermost part of the eye from its outer covering. This usually occurs as a result of severe trauma.

Second-degree burn: a type of burn that involves the entire epidermis and part of the dermis; also known as a partial thickness burn.

Seizure: a result of a sudden disturbance in brain function; it may be partial or generalized depending on how much of the brain is affected.

Shock: a condition resulting from circulatory system failure. It must be treated immediately because it can quickly lead to unconsciousness and death.

Simple fracture: a type of fracture where the bone is broken into no more than two pieces.

Skin elasticity: the ability of the skin to stretch.

Splint: a rigid bandage used to keep movement to a minimum in cases of dislocations and fractures.

Sprain: a condition that results from torn or stretched ligaments, tendons, and blood vessels around joints.

Stabilized: a condition that is not changing and one in which the victim is not in immediate danger of dying.

Status epilepticus: a condition that is marked by seizures occurring one after another with little or no rest in between.

Sternum: breastbone.

Strain: a condition that results from torn or stretched muscles around joints.

Stupor: a state of reduced consciousness.

Superficial burn: a burn that involves only the epidermis; also known as a first-degree burn.

Support: being able to transport a cat so the spinal column stays straight.

Tendon: the fibrous structure that attaches muscle to bone.

Thiamine: a B-complex vitamin necessary for normal nervous system activity; also known as vitamin B_1.

Third-degree burn: a burn that involves the entire thickness of the skin; also known as a full thickness burn.

Third eyelid: a membrane that lies between the lower lid and the surface of the eye and that may move to cover the surface of the eye.

Thromboembolism: obstruction of a blood vessel with a clot formed in the heart or another blood vessel.

Tourniquet: a very constrictive band that is applied as a last resort to stop severe bleeding.

Transport: a technique of moving a cat safely without causing further injury.

Triage: a technique that involves making a quick assessment of the major problems and sorting these problems from most severe to least severe.

Umbilicus: navel; the site where the umbilical cord was attached to the fetus; located in the midabdomen.

Urethra: the tube that connects the bladder to the external opening.

Urethral plug: an obstructive mass composed of matrix material mixed with mineral salts and found in the urethra.

Urinary tract blockage: a condition that most commonly occurs when the urethra becomes obstructed.

Urolith: a small stone composed of mineral salts that forms in the urinary tract and may cause blockage.

Vestibular syndrome: a disorder that occurs suddenly, has no known cause, and affects the sense of balance.

Vulva: the external opening of the female genital tract.

Wheeze: a whistling sound heard during breathing.

Index